# CONTENTS

# INTRODUCTION

The very first piece of old carnival glass that I bought was an Imperial piece. I actually bought four pieces of carnival that day back in 1969, but the first one was an Imperial's Fashion breakfast creamer, in smoke. I paid the sum of $3.50 for it, quite a bargain even at the low price levels then. At that time, my mother was just starting out with her own carnival glass collection, so I decided to tuck the little creamer away and give it to her as a Christmas present. It took her nearly six years to find the matching breakfast sugar, and I remember how thrilled she was when she finally did.

*Fashion breakfast creamer in smoke.*

My mother passed away in 1988, and her, by then, impressive collection was sold by Tom Burns at an auction. I remember a little lump swelling up in my throat as that little two-piece breakfast set came up for sale. It brought an astounding $450.00, a record price for one of those sets, unsurpassed to this day.

In September of 1994, I attended the New England Carnival Glass Association Convention as their guest speaker. There, on one of the tables of glass for sale, sat a little smoke Fashion breakfast creamer. It was priced at $35.00, a bargain at today's price levels. I thought of my mother, and reached for my wallet. That little creamer now sits in my collection. In fact, it is pictured in this book. I can't help wondering if it will take me six years to find the matching sugar. Probably not. Today, it will likely take twice that long, if indeed I ever find it at all.

I guess that because of the little breakfast set I have always had a soft spot in my heart for Imperial's carnival glass, even though it has had its ups and downs in collector popularity over the years. Many collectors tend to shy away from Imperial's carnival glass, for a variety of reasons. To my way of thinking, none of them are valid.

Most of the carnival glass producing firms chose floral, naturalistic, and stylized designs in fanciful, decorative shapes as their major themes. Imperial went a different route, producing functional, utilitarian shapes, using geometric or "near cut" designs as their predominant theme, and these types of shapes and patterns have never been among the most popular with collectors. I have never really understood this. Imperial produced a quality of glass that was in many ways far superior to that of their competitors. When you combine this with the intricate detail of their mold work and the brilliant, multicolor, radium iridescence that they alone were capable of achieving, you have an example of the glassmaker's art of matchless beauty. In my opinion, Imperial produced the most beautiful purple carnival glass and the richest, most vibrant marigold color of any of the carnival glass producers, bar none.

Perhaps it is because of the extensive reproductions of Imperial carnival glass that collectors shy away from it. I have never really understood this, either. Nearly all of the new carnival glass that Imperial produced between 1962 and 1985 is clearly trademarked to distinguish it from the old.

After the publication of my book on Northwood's carnival glass, I received a great deal of correspondence from carnival glass collectors all over the country. Many of them specifically asked if I was planning to do a book on Imperial's carnival glass and if so, when this would occur. It was then that I began to realize the real reason why so many collectors seem to place Imperial's carnival glass on the back shelf, so to speak. They are simply not that familiar with it! Over the years, carnival glass collectors have been hit with a constant barrage of books, information, and publicity touting the merits of Northwood, Fenton, and Millersburg carnival glass. Almost nothing has been done on Imperial. It has lived in the shadow of the aforementioned firms for far too long, and it is time to change this.

Collecting Imperial's carnival glass offers many exciting advantages, especially for the collector who is just starting out. Many of the shapes and patterns can still be found without too much difficulty and at affordable prices. An impressive collection of Imperial carnival can be put together without taking out a second mortgage on your home. Old Imperial carnival glass has everything going for it. It offers tremendous variety of pattern and shapes, superior quality glass, and often exceptional iridescence. It has now been over ten years since Imperial closed its doors. All of the glass produced there, old and new, has become a sought-after collectible. As time passes, Imperial glass of all types will prove to be a wise investment. So my advice to any novice collector is simple and straightforward: Imperial's carnival glass — go for it!

Carl O. Burns
July, 1995

# THE IMPERIAL GLASS COMPANY
## 1901 – 1985

In 1901, the area around southeastern Ohio, western Pennsylvania, and the northwest corner of West Virginia was the hub of the glassmaking industry in America. From Pittsburgh westward, the Ohio River Valley was lined with glass factories. The area around Bellaire, Ohio, alone, was home to nearly a dozen of them. Just over the river in Wheeling, West Virginia, Harry Northwood was establishing his new venture in the old Hobbs factory. Some 50 miles to the west, at Cambridge, Ohio, a new factory was being built by the National Glass Company. To organize yet another glassmaking concern in the face of such stiff competition would surely be quite a gamble. Yet, that's exactly what a group of Bellaire, Ohio, and Wheeling, West Virginia, investors did that year when the Imperial Glass Company of Bellaire, Ohio, was formed.

After nearly three years of preparation and construction, the new factory was finally ready. The first glass was made on January 13, 1904. From the very start, Imperial's aim was to produce a superior quality glass that would be affordable to the mass-market consumer. F.W. Woolworth Company became their first customer, placing an order with Imperial to supply nearly 500 stores. The fine quality crystal table sets, berry sets, water sets, and utilitarian serving pieces that Imperial produced for them became an instant success. Large orders from two other mass-market retailers, McCrory's and Kresge's, soon followed. The items that Imperial supplied to these three firms were of a fine, pressed crystal, superior in quality to the wares made by most of Imperial's competitors. It was this dedication to affordable quality that was to become the hallmark of Imperial's success.

The era of the glass that we have come to call Carnival began during the winter of 1907 – 1908 when the Fenton Art Glass Company introduced their first iridescent lines. Harry Northwood jumped on the iridescent glass bandwagon later in 1908. By the following year, Dugan, Westmoreland, Millersburg, and Imperial had followed suit. The first documented appearance of Imperial's carnival glass in wholesale catalogs occurred in 1910. It would continue to appear in them until as late as 1930.

During this 20-year period, Imperial applied their same high-quality standards to their iridescent lines. The brilliant, multicolor, radium iridescence that they produced was never equaled by any of their competitors. They produced a richer, more vibrant marigold color and a deeper, more uniform shade of purple than any other carnival glass-producing firm. Unique to Imperial's iridescent line was a color that they called Sapphire. This color is called smoke by today's collectors. Other firms, including Northwood, tried to duplicate it, but with little success. Helios, a light to medium green glass with a silver/gold iridescent sheen was another Imperial creation. The color called Clambroth, a light, ginger-ale colored glass, with a delicate, pastel iridescence was another Imperial innovation.

Imperial expanded their production of iridescent glass in 1916 with the introduction of their stretch glass line, called Imperial Jewels. Much of this ware is trademarked with the famous Imperial cross mark. Iridescent production was expanded even further in 1922 when Imperial introduced a new line called Free Hand. The Free Hand ware was a line of hand-blown, crystal, cased, and colored glass, some of which was iridized. It was made by a group of European glass artisans, brought by Imperial to this country. It is eagerly sought by art glass enthusiasts today.

The stock market crash of 1929 hit the glass houses of the Ohio River Valley, including Imperial, especially hard. Because of the ensuing rapid rise of inflation rates, much of the mass market was soon lost to inexpensive foreign imports. One by one, the majority of the glass factories in the Ohio River Valley folded. In 1931 Imperial, too, filed for Chapter 11. It was only through the efforts of its court-appointed receivers that the company was able to weather the storm of the Great Depression.

During these lean years, Imperial revived many of the molds used for carnival production, incorporating them into the lines of pastel pink, blue, and green glass that has come to be called Depression glass. New lines in frosted crystal and opaque milk glass also helped to pull the firm through the tough times. Then, during the 1930s, Imperial received an order from the Quaker Oats Company for a new line of premium glassware. In many ways, this new line, and another soon to follow, would be the company's salvation. The new line was called Cape Cod, and it became one of the Imperial's all-time bestsellers. The second new line, introduced in 1937, was called Candlewick. It was to become an even greater success. Production of the design continued in varying degrees for nearly 40 years. To this day it remains one of the most popular patterns in American glass history.

The years from 1940 to 1960 were ones of prosperity, expansion, and acquisition for Imperial. They purchased the famous Central Glass Works of Wheeling, West Virginia, in 1940. The year 1958 saw the purchase of the molds from the recently closed Heisey Glass Company. Two years later, the molds of the Cambridge Glass Company followed. Many of the Heisey and Cambridge molds were revived in the 1960s for production in many types of glass. Included among these were the famous Heisey figural animals. "Heisey By Imperial" became a staple part of the line.

Something else happened in the early 1960s. Interest in the iridescent glass that we call carnival began to grow. Long forgotten, tucked away in attics and cellars, the iridescent glass produced early in this century began to re-emerge onto the collector's market. In 1962, Imperial made their first re-issues of their original carnival glass patterns and shapes. The second great era of carnival glass production was underway. Many carnival glass collecting purists were horrified at these reproductions. However, it was these reproductions that would play a major role in the expansion of interest in the *old* glass. As a result of them, a whole new generation was introduced to carnival glass.

In the early 1960s, Imperial also revived another long-forgotten form of the glassmaker's art: slag glass. No major glasshouse had produced it in any quantity since the early 1900s. Purple slag, introduced in 1959, followed by caramel slag, in 1964, proved to be very popular sellers for Imperial. Ruby slag was first made in 1969, and jade slag was added to the line in the 1970s. These lines have already become some of the rapidly rising stars of the collectible glass market.

The 1970s brought a major change for Imperial. On December 19, 1972, Imperial was sold to Lenox Inc. of New Jersey. They became a wholly owned subsidiary of Lenox, and the name of the company was officially changed to IGC Liquidating Corporation. Production of glass continued, but this change of ownership really marked a turning point for Imperial. It began the final decade of glass production.

In 1981, Imperial was sold to a private investor, Arthur Lorch. Production of glass continued, but the handwriting was on the wall. The following year, Imperial was again sold to another private investor, Robert Stahl. This venture was also short lived, and in 1984 Mr. Stahl declared bankruptcy. The Imperial molds were sold and the company closed its doors on April 11, 1985, at 5:00 p.m. The vacant factory was sold to Anna Maroon of Bellaire, Ohio, who took possession of it on April 22, 1985.

Then in September of 1986, a Moundsville, West Virginia, newspaper reported that Ms. Maroon had leased a portion of the factory to four glass artisans: Bradford Law, Fred Wilkerson, Harold Logsdon, and Bob Simsa. All four of these men had worked at the Fostoria Glass Company. They had formed a partnership and were intending to manufacture glass at the Imperial factory. Reportedly, a neeling oven, a "glory hole," and a 300 pound capacity melting tank were already completed. The four men had already acquired some 35 to 40 molds, and were looking to purchase and create more. They named this new venture The Pioneer Glass Company. This company did produce some glass, including a special line made from old Imperial Mount Vernon pattern molds. These items had the logo "Save Imperial" molded on them. They also produced figural glass animals from molds of their own creation. Sadly, this venture was also short lived, lasting only two years.

So the curtain came down on the final act at the Imperial Glass Company of Bellaire, Ohio. One of the oldest surviving glasshouses of America was no more. But production of beautiful glass had lived there for over 83 years, leaving new generations of collectors some of the finest quality glass ever produced to collect, preserve, and enjoy for many decades to come.

# IMPERIAL'S CARNIVAL PRODUCTION

From the very first day of production, the ethic of the artisans at Imperial was to produce a superior quality glass at a price affordable to the mass-market consumer. In this, they certainly succeeded. This dedication to a high quality product was carried over to the production of their iridescent lines.

In recent years much of the attention and publicity in carnival glass collecting circles has centered on the glass produced by Northwood and Fenton. I would certainly not deny the fact that both of these firms produced a much wider variety of stylized and naturalistic patterns than did Imperial. Nor would I deny the tremendous appeal that these types of designs hold with collectors. However, as far as the actual quality of the glass is concerned, Imperial's product was superior to that which was made by either of these firms. It was a thicker, heavier glass of unmatched clarity, brilliance, and depth of color. The sharpness and definition of the molding is also of superior quality. It was obviously a far more expensive glass to produce while maintaining competitiveness in the market. In this respect, Imperial succeeded where other "high quality" glasshouses, such as Millersburg, failed.

Not only was the glass that Imperial produced of a superior quality, but also the iridescence that they applied to it. They produced a richer, more brilliant marigold color than any of their competitors. The beautifully blended tones of the multicolor, radium iridescence that they achieved is often dazzling. But it is their purple carnival glass that is, in this writer's opinion, the ultimate expression of carnival glass artistry. No other carnival glass producer could equal the majestic lustre that Imperial was capable of producing on their purple carnival glass. Anyone who has ever held in their hands a purple Colonial Lady vase, or a Diamond Lace pitcher, will know what I am talking about. While the quality of the iridescence on the glass made by Imperial's competitors can vary from poor to outstanding, you will rarely see a poorly iridized piece of Imperial carnival glass.

While the earliest documented appearance of Imperial's carnival glass in the wholesale catalogs was in 1910, the firm was producing it by 1909. Surviving letters, dated 1909, specifically refer to the production of iridescent glass at Northwood, Fenton, and Imperial. The letters concern an agreement between the management at these factories and the members of the American Flint Glass Workers Union. The letters specifically mention Local #13, and this was the Union Chapter that the workers at Imperial belonged to.

The carnival glass produced by Imperial is unique in many respects. A large percentage of the carnival glass produced by Northwood, Fenton, Dugan, and Millersburg is primarily decorative in nature. They made tremendous quantities of ruffled bowls, handled bon-bons, stemmed compotes, and whimsical shapes. Imperial chose to follow a different path with their iridescent production. A large portion of their carnival production was devoted to functional, utilitarian shapes such as water sets, berry sets, milk pitchers, serving trays, candlesticks, pickle dishes, goblets, and wine sets. They produced comparatively few decorative shapes such as stemmed compotes, handled bon-bons, and the like. This is the main reason why Imperial produced a thicker, heavier quality of glass. They were not made to be placed on a shelf and looked at. The were made to be used.

Surviving factory catalogs provide some unique insight into the carnival glass colors that Imperial produced. Most of the carnival glass producing firms gave their wares color names based on the base color of the glass. Imperial did not. Most of the color names that they used were based on the types of iridescent treatment applied to the glass rather than the actual color of the glass itself. Often the color names that they used had nothing to do with the base color of the glass. This practice has caused considerable confusion over the years. Many early carnival glass researchers consequently misidentified several of Imperial's carnival colors. Sorting it all out is not unlike translating from one language to another, and then having to translate that to yet a third.

The following is a listing of carnival glass colors that appeared in an Imperial factory catalog from the carnival production era.

PEACOCK — This glass has a very brilliant iridescence, but the effect is not loud. Every color of the rainbow is represented, a golden yellow predominating. Many color variations.

RUBIGOLD — Our famous dark red iridescent glass, with tints of other colors. The biggest selling line of iridescent glass in the world.

NURUBY — Very similar to Rubigold, but because used mostly on plain designs, a slight change in the chemicals is necessary.

SAPPHIRE — A dark, blue-gray iridescent color on crystal glass. An entirely new, expensive-looking effect.

AZUR — A very brilliant iridescent effect on dark amethyst-colored glass. All colors of the rainbow such as yellow, green, and rose combine in this treatment.

PURPLE GLAZE — A very brilliant blue iridescent effect on dark amethyst glass. The effect is similar to that of the plain blue iridescence on the expensive lead-lustre glass.

HELIOS — A silvery iridescence on green glass. Very beautiful.

BLUE GLOW & RED GLOW — Similar to Nuruby and Sapphire.

From these descriptions, it becomes quite clear that Imperial's color names were based on the type of iridescent treatment rather than on the base glass color. The colors listed as Azur and Purple Glaze are good illustrations of this. Since both are described as being on amethyst glass, the actual color name *must* refer to the iridescent treatment. Azur refers to the multi-color iridescence, while Purple Glaze surely refers to the brilliant, electric blue iridescent treatment that is sometimes found on examples of Imperial's purple carnival.

The color listed as Helios is another good example. The name comes from the Greek god of the sun. Literally translated, it means "brilliant radiance." Since the sun is certainly not green, we know that the color listed as Helios refers to the silver/gold iridescent treatment, and not specifically to the base color of the glass. Granted, this type of iridescence is most often found on light to medium green glass; however, examples in other colors such as amber, olive, amethyst, and even smoke are sometimes found with this silver/gold helios iridescence.

The color listed as Rubigold, despite its description, does *not* refer to red carnival glass! Imperial consistently used this name to market their marigold carnival glass.

It has long been accepted that the name Peacock refers to the carnival color that we call smoke today. However, the description listed for the color called Sapphire certainly seems to be a much more likely candidate for the color known as smoke. It is interesting to note that virtually no specific base glass color is mentioned in the description of the name Peacock. There are a couple of possibilities here. It may well refer to the carnival color that we call clambroth. The description does state that a golden yellow predominates, and many examples of clambroth carnival glass have a strong yellow tone in the iridescence. The last three words in the description, "many color variations," lead to a second possibility. The term Peacock may simply refer to a type of iridescent treatment that was applied to any one of several different base glass colors.

We have nine color descriptions above from an Imperial factory catalog. Yet, Imperial is known to have produced carnival glass on no less than 23 different base glass colors. So it becomes even more obvious that many of these color descriptions refer to different types of iridescent treatment that could have been, and probably were, applied to many different base glass colors.

The catalog also describes several satin iridescent effects, all with a "crizzled, very dainty, modest color effect." The colors are listed as Iris Ice, Rose Ice, Blue Ice, Amber Ice, Green Ice, and Amethyst Ice. These are undoubtedly stretch glass colors. The word "crizzled" refers to the onion-skin effect of stretch iridescence.

It is also nearly impossible to pin down the dates that most of Imperial's carnival colors first appeared. Most of the surviving factory catalogs are numbered, but not dated. The various Imperial carnival colors appear in the Butler Brothers Wholesale Catalogs quite sporadically, on a on again — off again basis. So it seems likely that Imperial produced all of their carnival colors, in varying degrees, throughout the entire span between 1909 and 1930. Some of the colors that Imperial is known to have produced *never do* appear in the wholesale catalogs. It is very possible and even likely that some of these colors were made on a special order or limited edition basis for specific customers, and not marketed through the general wholesale distributors. F.W. Woolworth, McCrory, and Kresge were all big Imperial customers and no doubt some of Imperial's carnival lines were made exclusively for them. Glasshouses often made specific items and colors exclusively for certain customers, and they still do so today. This may well account for the rarity of certain shapes and colors on today's market. Imperial's Cobalt Blue and Emerald Green carnival is extremely rare and found only on a very limited number of shapes and patterns. It may well have been made in relatively small amounts for a specific customer.

At this point, it is *very* important to take note of a situation that is unique to Imperial. They produced three distinct types of green carnival glass, all with different iridescent treatments. There is a world of difference between them as to rarity, desirability, and value. Helios is a light to medium shade of green with a predominantly silver/gold iridescent sheen. There is a little, if any, multicolor lustre in the iridescence. It is the most easily found, and least popular of the three. Emerald is a very dark, rich green with a dazzling, radium, almost "electric" iridescence. It is extremely rare, ranks very high in desirability, and always commands premium prices. Somewhere in between falls the color called, simply, green. This is a medium shade of green with a metallic, multicolor, satin iridescent lustre. It is found in a fairly extensive variety of patterns and shapes.

The longevity of carnival glass production at Imperial was surpassed only by that of the Diamond Glass Company. Diamond's carnival lines continued to appear in the wholesale catalogs until the spring of 1931. The final curtain call of Imperial's carnival glass appeared in the October 1930 Butler Brother catalog. There is an assortment of Floral and Optic pieces in assorted iridescent colors. There are also two sizes of marigold bowls in the Lustre Rose and Heavy Grape patterns. Of particular interest are the wholesale prices quoted for these assortments. Just 16 years earlier, in 1914, these Lustre Rose and Heavy Grape bowls could be purchased for 79 cents per dozen. The price for the same bowls in 1930 was an astounding $3.95 per dozen. That's five times the price in less than a generation. It is easy to see the devastating effect that the skyrocketing inflation of the stock market crash had on the glass industry in America. Less that one year after this final appearance of Imperial's carnival glass, the company had filed for Chapter 11 and was operating under receivership. They would survive the rough waters of the Great Depression, but it marked the end of the first great era of carnival glass. Some sporadic production of iridescent glass took place there between 1931 and 1959, but it was not until the 1960s that any further major production runs of the glass we call carnival occurred.

## TRADEMARKS ON OLD IMPERIAL CARNIVAL GLASS

Between 1904 and 1921 Imperial filed for patents on no less than five different trademarks. Only three of these are found on old Imperial carnival pieces and only very rarely. These three marks are illustrated here:

The stylized Nuart trademark is found primarily on chop plates in the Homestead and Chryanthemum patterns. The word Nuart may also be found molded in block letters around the collar fitting ring of some of Imperial's carnival light shades. The Nucut trademark was used exclusively on a line of geometric-type designs made primarily in non-iridized crystal; however, on rare occasions some of these pieces are found in marigold carnival.

The other trademark shown is commonly referred to as the Imperial Cross Mark. It is sometimes found on items in the Optic & Buttons, Wide Panel, Colonial, and Imperial's Grape patterns. It also appears on items in the Imperial Jewels stretch glass lines.

Virtually all other *old* Imperial carnival glass is not trademarked in any manner. The well-known, superimposed IG trademark is *not* an old mark. This trademark was not adopted until 1951, and all carnival glass bearing this mark was made after 1961.

# ORIGINAL IMPERIAL PATTERN NUMBERS

Fortunately for collectors and researchers, several copies of Imperial factory catalogs from the carnival production era have survived the years. As a result, we know many of the original pattern numbers of the glass that Imperial produced. We even know the number of the first design that Imperial made. The pattern known to carnival collectors as Three In One is listed in the catalogs as Imperial's #1. It was made in non-iridized crystal, in a wide variety of shapes, staring in 1904. The molds were used for carnival production beginning in 1910, and the pattern appears in the earliest documented assortment of Imperial carnival glass to be found in a Butler Brothers Wholesale Catalog from the same year.

One area concerning these original pattern numbers is a confusing and often frustrating one. Because the majority of Imperial's carnival patterns are exterior surface designs, these factory designation numbers are based on the exterior pattern even when they are combined with a more prominent interior design. For example, the pattern known to carnival glass collectors as Flute #1 is actually Imperial's #700 pattern. This same pattern was used as the exterior on Imperial's Heavy Grape pieces. Thus, both patterns carry the designation of Imperial's #700 in the factory catalogs.

Perhaps the best example to illustrate the confusion that this practice can cause can be found with regard to two other well-known Imperial patterns. The Floral and Optic pattern carries the designation of Imperial's #514. When combined with the Double Dutch interior pattern, the piece is still illustrated in the catalog as Imperial's #514. To add to the confusion, Imperial's Windmill pattern, which is really the same pattern line as Double Dutch, also carries the designation of Imperial's #514, even though it does not carry the Floral and Optic exterior design. If you think that's confusing, just wait. There's more. A fourth digit was often added to the number to designate shape. The Windmill milk pitcher carries the designation #5142; the water pitcher, #5143; the 5" ruffled sauce dish, #5145, etc.

Sorting this all out can be a real headache. This is especially so when one attempts to sort out all of the various Flute, Colonial, and Wide Panel type patterns. Imperial made carnival versions of no less than six of these designs, all with different production numbers. To make matters worse, some of the sets in these designs were made up of items with different pattern numbers.

So of the 100+ carnival patterns that Imperial produced, I have been able to track down close to 50 of the original pattern numbers. Where known, they appear in the text for the appropriate designs.

# ORIGINAL IMPERIAL FACTORY CATALOGS 1909 – 1930

The following pages are selections of Imperial's carnival glass taken from old Imperial factory catalogs from the carnival glass production era. They offer some interesting insights into the manufacture and marketing of old carnival glass.

Of particular interest is the page from catalog #300 labeled "FOUR SEVENTY FOUR, STAR MEDALLION, FLUTE AND CANE" (page 24). There are items from several other pattern lines included in this assortment. In the second row is a Star and File tall sundae. This catalog page proves that this item was made in carnival, yet to date no examples have surfaced.

Another page offers seven different stemware pieces in the Smooth Rays pattern (page 22). Not all of these are yet known, but were obviously made.

On some of these pages you will find references to colors called red glow and blue glow. These are the names given to the reformulated colors that we call marigold and smoke.

## THREE BRIGHT IRIDESCENT COLORS.

RUBIGOLD — SAPPHIRE — PEACOCK.

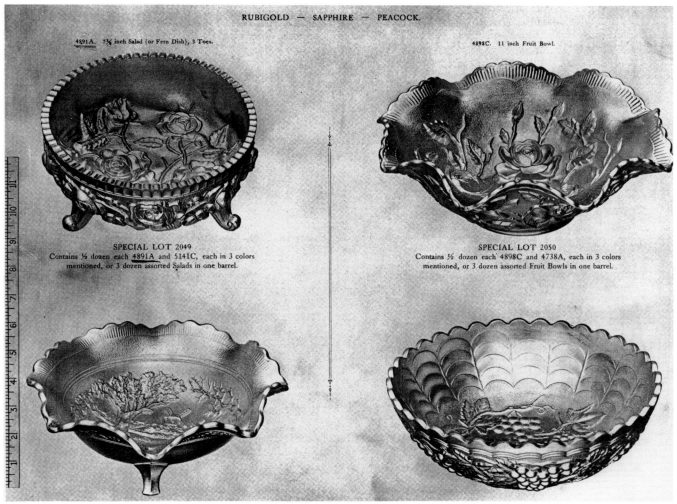

4891A.   7½ inch Salad (or Fern Dish), 3 Toes.

4898C.   11 inch Fruit Bowl.

SPECIAL LOT 2049
Contains ½ dozen each 4891A and 5141C, each in 3 colors mentioned, or 3 dozen assorted Salads in one barrel.

SPECIAL LOT 2050
Contains ½ dozen each 4898C and 4738A, each in 3 colors mentioned, or 3 dozen assorted Fruit Bowls in one barrel.

5141C.   9 inch Salad, 3 Toes.

For Colors See Page 3 of this Book

4738A.   9 inch Fruit Bowl.

15

**SPECIAL LOT 2095**
Contains 1 dozen assorted Footed Bowls
No. 600B, or ⅓ dozen each
**NURUBY, SAPPHIRE AND PEACOCK**

600B.   11 inch Footed Bowl.

5145A.   4¾ inch Berry.

5145C.   5½ inch Berry.

4735A.   4¾ inch Berry.

4895C.   5½ inch Berry.

4895A.   4¾ inch Berry.

4735C.   5½ inch Berry.

**SPECIAL LOT 2101**
Contains 21 dozen assorted Berries, or 1 dozen each
of 7 Berries, illustrated, each in 3 colors:
**NURUBY — SAPPHIRE — PEACOCK.**

2565/3C.   5½ inch Berry.

For colors see Page 3 of this Book.

3 Different Colors (Rubigold — Azur — Helios) in one barrel.

L2567/3C.  9 inch Berry.
Azur.

M465.  7½ inch Salad.
Rubigold.

K7007/4A.  9 inch Berry.
Helios.

K4897A.  8 inch Berry.
Helios.

M496C.  9 inch Berry.
Rubigold.

Each article can be ordered separately, see Price List.

# 18 PIECE BUFFET SET.

Bright Rubigold Color only.

SPECIAL LOT 1908 contains ⅓ dozen each of 4 piece Tea Set, 7 piece Berry Set and 7 piece Water Set, or 1 dozen Assorted Sets, RUBIGOLD only.

M489.  Spoon Holder.
1 in Set.

M489.  Sugar and Cover.
1 in Set.

M489.  Cream.
1 in Set.

EACH SET AND EACH ARTICLE IN EACH
SET CAN BE BOUGHT SEPARATELY.

M4895A.  4¾ inch Berry.
6 in Set.

M489.  Butter and Cover.
1 in Set.

M489.  Tumbler.
6 in Set.

M4898A.  9 inch Berry.
1 in Set.

M489.  Pitcher.
1 in Set.

Barrels are Charged Extra.

## RED GLOW.    BLUE GLOW.

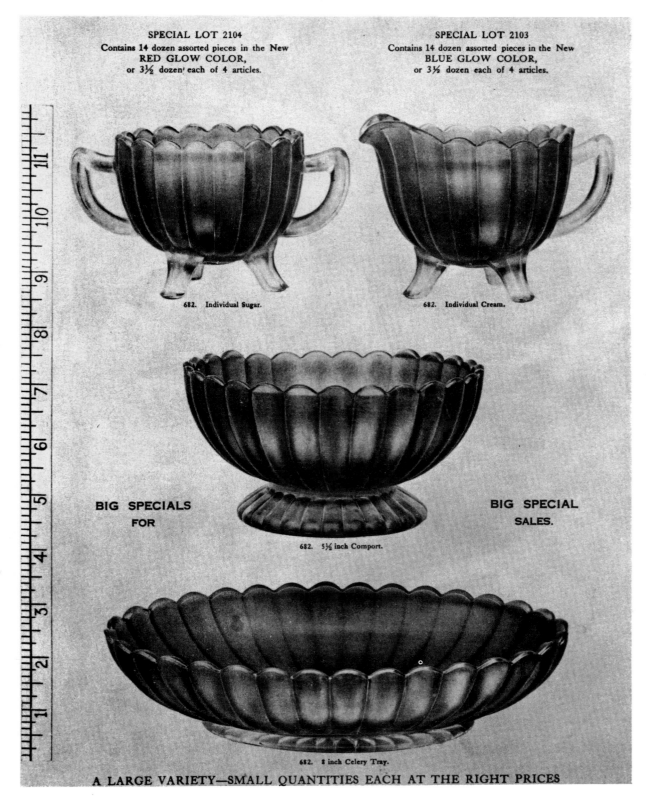

**SPECIAL LOT 2104**
Contains 14 dozen assorted pieces in the New
RED GLOW COLOR,
or 3½ dozen each of 4 articles.

**SPECIAL LOT 2103**
Contains 14 dozen assorted pieces in the New
BLUE GLOW COLOR,
or 3½ dozen each of 4 articles.

682.   Individual Sugar.

682.   Individual Cream.

BIG SPECIALS
FOR

BIG SPECIAL
SALES.

682.   5½ inch Comport.

682.   8 inch Celery Tray.

## A LARGE VARIETY—SMALL QUANTITIES EACH AT THE RIGHT PRICES

### THAT IS THE RESULT OF OUR SPECIAL LOTS.

# SPECIAL LOT 2045. RUBIGOLD WATER SETS.

This Lot contains ¼ dozen each of the 4 Water Sets illustrated, or 1 dozen assorted 7 piece Sets in one barrel.

M484. Tumbler.  M484. ½ Gallon Pitcher.  M514. Tumbler.  M5143. ½ Gallon Pitcher.

EACH WATER SET
Consists of One Pitcher and Six Tumblers.

M670. Tumbler.  M670. ½ Gallon Pitcher.  M474. Tumbler.  M4743. ½ Gallon Pitcher.

Every Item Shown in this Book can be Ordered Separately.

# BRIGHT IRIDESCENT. RUBIGOLD ONLY.

M600. Table Salt.  M600. Tooth Pick.  M6000. 3½ inch Sherbet.  M6001. 4 inch Ice Cream.  M399/1. 3 inch Sherbet.

M755/1. Custard Cup.  M672. Custard Cup.  M666. Low Ice Cream on M666—6 inch Plate. (2 Pieces)  M5822B. Cup and Saucer. (2 Pieces)

M593. Child's Mug.  M5821. Cafe Parfait.  M612. Tall Ice Cream on M612—6 inch Plate  M600. 10 oz. Lemonade Glass.

21

# BRIGHT IRIDESCENT.   RUBIGOLD ONLY.

M442/1
1 oz. Cordial.
2 dozen.

M442/1
2 oz. Wine.
2 dozen.

M442/1
3 oz. Wine.
1 dozen.

M442/1
4 oz. Claret.
1 dozen.

M442/1
6 oz. Champagne.
1 dozen.

M442/1
9 oz. Goblet.
1 dozen.

M442/1
10 oz. Goblet.
1 dozen.

M666
1 oz. Cordial.
2 dozen.

M666
3 oz. Wine.
1 dozen.

M666
9 oz. Goblet.
1 dozen.

M9
1½ oz. Wine.
2 dozen.

M9
3 oz. Wine.
1 dozen.

M9
4 oz. Claret.
1 dozen.

M9
8 oz. Goblet.
1 dozen.

# FOR A SPECIAL SALE LOOK UP THE PRICE!

SNAP 14 contains ¾ dozen 8 piece Punch Sets, as illustrated (Bowl, Foot and Six Cups)

# FOUR SEVENTY FOUR    STAR MEDALLION
# FLUTE AND CANE

## Made Only in Rubigold Iridescent Glass

See pages 101 and 106 for pitchers to match tumblers and goblets.

M612. 6 inch Plate

M612B. 4½ inch Jelly or Fruit Salad

M612. 12 oz. Ice Tea

M612. 10 oz. Table Tumbler

M612. 9 oz. Goblet

M612. 2 oz. Wine

M612. 1 oz. Cordial

M612. 6 inch Plate
Fits under:
Jelly or Fruit Salad
12 oz. Ice Tea Tumbler
10 oz. Table Tumbler
9 oz. Goblet
3¾ inch Low Sherbet
3¾ inch Tall Sundae

M612L. 5½ inch Low Sherbet

M612L. 3½ inch Tall Sundae

M666B. 4½ inch Jelly or Fruit Salad

M666. 3½ inch Sherbet

M666. 6 inch Plate

M666. 6 inch Plate
Fits under:
4½ inch Jelly or Fruit Salad
3½ inch Sherbet
12 oz. Ice Tea Tumbler
9 oz. Table Tumbler

M474. 6 oz. Custard

M474. 4 inch Sherbet

M474. ¾ oz. Cordial

M474. 2 oz. Wine

M474. 8 oz. Goblet

M666. 12 oz. Ice Tea

M666. 9 oz. Table Tumbler

M3457B. 7-piece Sundae or Ice Cream Set
Diameter of Bowl 9 inches, Sherbets 4 inches

M670. 10 oz. Mug

M473. Cup and Saucer

M473. 10 oz. Goblet

M473. 2 oz. Wine

Catalog No. 300      Illustrations ½ Size      Imperial Glassware

# IMPERIAL CARNIVAL GLASS EXPORTS

Imperial is known to have produced a considerable quantity of carnival glass for export to overseas markets. A large percentage of the exports went to Europe via England. A company called Market & Co. Ltd. was their importing agent, starting about 1911. Johnsen & Jorgensen Flint Glass Ltd. of Farringdon Street, London, was one of the retail and wholesale distributors for Imperial Glass.

Subsequently, as least two European glass companies are known to have produced carnival glass copies of several Imperial patterns. This occurred in the mid 1920s to the early 1930s. The Sowerby Glassworks of Gateshead, England, produced a version of the Scroll Embossed pattern. Examples can sometimes be found with the Sowerby "Peacock's Head" trademark. The Eda Glassworks of Sweden copied the Tiger Lily and Curved Star patterns. In fact, they made a more extensive line of Curved Star than did the pattern's creator, Imperial. This line included butter dishes, creamers, sugars, chalice-like vases, and an impressive, single-lily Epergne.

Imperial carnival glass was also exported to the Central and South American countries. Items in the Frosted Block and Star Medallion patterns were among the most prolific of these. Some examples of these patterns can be found with the words, "Made in U.S.A." molded in block letters around the inner lip of the collar base. These were pieces earmarked for export to Central and South America. Obviously, some of them either never made it there, or found their way back to the United States.

Imperial carnival glass also turns up in Australia. Whether it was shipped there from this country or found its way down under via shipments from England is uncertain.

# WHOLESALE CATALOGS

One of the most important resources available to the glass researcher and collector is the wholesale catalogs from the carnival glass era. During that period much of the general merchandise of all types was supplied to the retail market by several huge wholesale outlets. Many of the catalogs from these wholesalers have survived the years to provide today's glass collectors with a wealth of information that would otherwise by unknown.

One of the largest of these wholesalers was the Butler Brothers Company. They operated showrooms and warehouses in New York, Chicago, St. Louis, Dallas, and Minneapolis. Their showroom and warehouse in Chicago covered nearly five acres! They were not the only such wholesale outlets. There were many other similar companies, including Charles Broadway Rouss, G. Sommers & Co., The Baltimore Bargain House, John M. Smith Merchandise Company, and Frank Miller's of New York. Most of these firms published wholesale catalogs which were supplied to retailers throughout the country. Every type of merchandise immaginable was offered in these catalogs including a wide variety of glassware.

Glassware was offered in assortments at wholesale prices. These assortments were not put together by the wholesaler, but were packed at the factory of their origin. This is what makes these catalogs so valuable to researchers today. With their aid, we have been able to discover the origins of many glass patterns that were previously of undetermined attribution.

We can use one of the patterns in this book as an example of this process. The carnival glass pattern known as Snow Fancy has, for many years, been credited to the McKee Glass Company. During the research for this book, I discovered an assortment of glass in a 1922

Butler Brothers catalog that included an example of this pattern. Also in this same assortment was an example of the Octagon pattern, one of the most well known Imperial designs. Since these assortments were packed at the factory of origin, there is now no question that Snow Fancy is an Imperial product and never saw the inside of the McKee factory!

These wholesalers issued updated catalogs on a monthly bases. To date, only about 100 issues of the catalogs from these various companies are known. The carnival glass production era spanned almost 23 years. If just the three largest wholesalers each issued a monthly catalog during this time span, that comes to 828 issues! So you can see that there are still huge gaps in our knowledge of the distribution of carnival glass. We have only just begun to scratch the surface and have a long way to go.

Throughout this book, you will find assortments of Imperial's carnival glass that were taken directly from these wholesale catalogs.

# IMPERIAL CARNIVAL GLASS COLORS

Listed here are the names and descriptions of the carnival glass colors that Imperial is known to have produced. These names and descriptions refer to the base color of the glass and not to the colors of the iridescent treatment that was applied to them. The names of the colors are those that are used by carnival glass collectors. Imperial glass purists may be horrified at this; however, the vast majority of those who are interested in Imperial's carnival glass are to be found in the ranks of carnival glass collectors. It is, therefore, only logical to use the terms and names that are most generally accepted by them.

MARIGOLD — Orange or clear glass with an orange iridescent treatment.

MARIGOLD ON MILK — An opaque white or off-white glass with a marigold iridescent overlay.

CLAMBROTH — A light, ginger-ale color with a pastel iridescence.

HELIOS — A light to medium shade of green with a silver/gold iridescent sheen.

GREEN — A medium green shade with a metallic, multicolor iridescence, often with an abundant gold tone.

EMERALD — A dark, rich, emerald green with a brilliant, radium, multicolor iridescent lustre.

ICE GREEN — A light, frosty, pastel green with a delicate, pastel iridescence.

LIME GREEN — A light yellow/green, usually found with a marigold iridescent overlay.

VASELINE — Yellow; often found with a marigold iridescent overlay.

OLIVE — Olive green.

AQUA — Turquoise or aqua-marine, with a stronger green tone.

TEAL — A turquoise blue/green color with a strong blue tone.

PURPLE — A deep, rich purple; amethyst.

LAVENDER — A light, delicate, pastel shade of purple with a pastel iridescence.

VIOLET — A pastel shade of purple with strong blue tones.

BLUE — A rich, royal blue; cobalt.

LIGHT BLUE/SMOKE BLUE — A light smokey blue color, often found with a light marigold iridescent overlay.

ICE BLUE — A light, frosty, pastel blue with a delicate pastel iridescence.

CELESTE BLUE — Darker than ice blue but lighter than cobalt. Usually found with a stretch iridescence.

WHITE — A frosty, translucent white with a delicate pastel iridescence.

RED — A deep, cherry red.

AMBERINA — Red shading to yellow.

AMBER — A deep, rich amber/honey color.

SMOKE — A light to medium charcoal gray color.

SMOKE ON MILK GLASS — Milk glass with a smoke iridescent overlay.

In order to simplify color listings, all references to purple include the color known as amethyst. Both were intended to be the same color at the time of manufacture. Slight variations in temperature and chemical mix when the batches of glass were made often resulted in slight color variations.

# NOTES ON COLORS AND RARITY

MARIGOLD — Imperial produced tremendous amounts of marigold carnival glass. With very few exceptions, all Imperial patterns can be found in this color. A few of the exceptions would include the Diamond Lace water pitcher, the Chatelaine water pitcher, and the Zippered Heart queen's vase. Some items are far more rare in marigold than they are in the other colors. A good example would be the Colonial Lady vase.

PURPLE/AMETHYST — Imperial's production of this color was far more limited than that of its competitors. Most patterns and shapes are quite difficult to find in purple. There are, of course, exceptions. Some of the more easily found purple items include bowls in the Imperial's Grape, Pansy, and Star of David patterns, most sizes of Ripple vases, the Diamond Lace water set, and small bowls and plates in the Heavy Grape pattern. Most of Imperial's geometric or near-cut patterns are very rare and desirable in purple.

HELIOS — Fairly large amounts of this color were produced, but the variety of shapes and patterns is curiously selective. Most of the naturalistic designs, such as Pansy, Imperial's Grape, Heavy Grape, and Lustre Rose, can be found in reasonable quantity in Helios. The geometric designs are rarely seen in it. Among today's collectors, it seems to be one of the least popular colors. Helios has a predominately silver/gold iridescent sheen with little, if any, multicolored lustre.

EMERALD — Very rare to extremely rare in all patterns and shapes. Imperial apparently produced very little of this color. It always commands premium prices. It is a dark, rich emerald green with a brilliant, radium, almost "electric" iridescence.

GREEN — This is a medium shade of green with a shiny, metallic iridescence, usually with good multicolor highlights and a fairly heavy gold lustre. It is found in a fairly wide variety of patterns and shapes. Items in the Heavy Grape pattern are found frequently in this shade of green.

COBALT BLUE — Here again, very rare to extremely rare in all patterns and shapes. The only item that is found with any reasonable frequency is the Lustre Rose Fernery. Most known examples of this color are found in the naturalistic designs. Any pieces in the geometric or near-cut type patterns would be *extremely* rare finds. Most of those types of patterns are virtually unknown in cobalt blue.

SMOKE — Am Imperial creation, this color is found in a fairly wide variety of shapes and patterns. The most frequently seen items include vases of most types, bowls and small pieces in the geometric designs, and novelty items. The larger items such as water sets and the punch sets are harder to find. This color is rapidly growing in popularity.

CLAMBROTH — This ginger-ale colored glass is also found in fair abundance. Items such as the Lustre Rose footed fruit bowl and pieces in the Star Medallion, Frosted Block, and Waffle Block patterns are plentiful. Here again, larger items, such as water sets and punch sets, are scarce, though not unknown.

WHITE — What a shame that Imperial made so little of this color. On the relatively few examples known the quality of the frost and iridescence is outstanding and even superior to that of their competitors. With very few exceptions, such as items in the Frosted Block pattern, examples of Imperial's white carnival are very rare.

AMBER — Imperial was by far the largest producer of this color. Items in Imperial's Grape, Pansy, Lustre Rose, and the Ripple vase seem to be the most often found. The geometric designs are rarely found in amber.

RED — Imperial produced very small amounts of true, red carnival. Items known include pieces in Floral and Optic, Lustre Rose, and the Fashion punch set (the only *old*, true, red carnival glass punch set).

Virtually all other Imperial carnival colors, including ice blue, ice green, teal, aqua, lavender, violet, vaseline, olive, and marigold on milk glass range from very scarce to extremely rare. They were apparently produced in very limited quantities, perhaps on a special order basis for a few specific customers.

# NOTES ON IMPERIAL CARNIVAL SHAPES

Imperial produced a wide variety of carnival glass shapes, but in contrast to those produced by their competitors, a large percentage of these shapes were of a functional, utilitarian nature. Unlike Northwood or Fenton, they made comparatively few decorative shapes, such as compotes or two-handled bon-bons. This is the primary reason why so much of Imperial's glass was a thicker, heavier grade of glass. The pieces were designed to be used. Thus, the bulk of Imperial's carnival production was geared to berry sets, punch sets, milk pitchers, wine sets, candlesticks, and a wider variety of stemware pieces, than any of their competitors.

Hopefully collectors will find the following notes and guidelines on Imperial's carnival shapes to be useful.

PLATES — These have always been among the most popular shapes with collectors. Imperial produced fewer of them than did Northwood or Fenton. With only a few exceptions, most Imperial carnival plates are rarely found. Some of the more easily found plates include the Heavy Grape 8" size in marigold, helios, or purple, the Imperial's Grape 9" and 6" sizes in marigold, and clambroth examples of Star Medallion and Smooth Rays. Most others range from scarce to extremely rare! Some of the rarest plates include Chrysanthemum, Homestead, and the large chop plates in just about any color or pattern. Most of Imperial's plates are very rare in purple.

PUNCH SETS — Imperial made a large array of punch sets, and most of them are quite available in marigold. Virtually all other colors in all of their punch set patterns are really quite rare.

WATER SETS — Here again, the majority of Imperial's carnival water sets are reasonably plentiful in marigold. Some, like the Windmill, Imperial's Grape, and Lustre Rose, are also still available in helios. The only purple water set that is still reasonably available is the Diamond Lace, and even this is becoming scarce. Virtually all other purple water sets and water sets in other colors are *very* rare.

MILK PITCHERS — Imperial produced more of these than any of the other carnival glass producers. Nearly all of them are quite available in marigold. All other colors are rare.

STEMWARE SHAPES — Here again, Imperial produced a wider variety of goblets, wines, clarets, cordials, and sherbets than did any other firm. Most are known only in marigold. The exception is the wine sets. Several of them are known in purple, helios, and other colors. They are rarely found in colors other than marigold. Virtually all of the clarets, champagnes, and tiny cordials are extremely rare.

TABLE SETS — Surprisingly, Imperial produced very few of them. Only a handful of patterns were made in table sets. All are very rare when found in any colors other than marigold.

BOWLS — These are the most available of all Imperial carnival shapes. The majority of them fall into the berry set category. Imperial made comparatively few decorative, collar based, low, ruffled bowls. Many of their bowl shapes are of the round, deep shape. Most all of their bowls are easily found in marigold. Many are also reasonably available in purple, amber, and helios. Cobalt blue and emerald bowls are extremely rare in all patterns.

VASES — This is one area that might surprise many collectors. With a few exceptions, such as vases in Ripple, Freefold, and a couple of others, most Imperial carnival vases are actually quite rare. In fact, they really produced far fewer vases than either Fenton or Northwood! Vases in Poppy Show, Scroll & Flower Panel, Loganberry, Colonial Lady, Three Row, Thumbprint & Ovals, and Four Seventy Four are all very rare in any color.

CANDLESTICKS — Imperial also made a greater variety of carnival glass candlesticks than any of the other manufacturers. With the exception of the Six-Sided and Crucifix designs, all are quite easily found in marigold. Candlesticks in virtually any other color are quite rare.

Imperial also produced a huge variety of serving pieces, such as handled pickle dishes and relishes and center handles servers. All are easily found in marigold and seldom seen in the other colors.

# IMPERIAL CARNIVAL GLASS REPRODUCTIONS AND TRADEMARKS

Perhaps no other type of collectible glassware has been so heavily reproduced and reissued as has Imperial's carnival glass. Many collectors still shy away from the old Imperial carnival because they are unsure of age. However, we should not fault Imperial for their decision to reissue many of their iridescent lines. Rather, we should applaud them for doing so. The first Imperial Carnival reissues of the early to mid 1960s were to prove instrumental to the rise in popularity of the *old* carnival glass. By that time we were at least two full generations removed from the production era of the old carnival glass. A large percentage of the population had never seen it, or had any idea of what it was. They saw this new carnival glass in the stores, and they liked it. When they learned that this was a reissue of a type of glass that had been extremely popular some 40 to 50 years earlier, their curiosity about the original glass was peaked. The rest, as they say, is history. Old carnival glass became, and remains, the most popular collectible glassware of all time.

Imperial was the first to reproduce carnival glass. The new carnival lines first appeared in 1962. Items in the Imperial's Grape, Lustre Rose, Windmill, and Octagon patterns were among the first of these reissues. All of the new pieces were clearly marked with the trademark that Imperial had adopted in 1951. This mark consists of a stylized capitol letter I, superimposed over a stylized capitol letter G. Any Imperial glass of any type that bears this IG trademark was manufactured *after* 1951.

Imperial Glass Company Trademark
1951 – 1972

Between 1962 and 1972, the carnival glass reproductions made by Imperial were signed with the above trademark. A wide variety of patterns, shapes, and colors were made. Many were re-issues of old Imperial carnival designs. Some were made from molds that Imperial had purchased from Heisey and Cambridge and had never been made in old carnival glass. Colors produced during this period included marigold, smoke, white, red, green, amber, ice blue, aurora jewels, and amethyst.

Apparently a few reproduction pieces did leave the factory without being trademarked, as I have seen some examples of this. Also, some unscrupulous parties purchased pieces of new Imperial carnival, ground off the trademark, and then tried to sell the glass as old. This practice continues today, but is not as widespread as it was in the late 1960s and early 1970s. One of the items that was a favorite for this practice is a new carnival Windmill water set, made with a most unusual treatment. They are marigold in color, but the oval panel containing the windmill scene is frosted and not iridized. I have seen several of these sets that have had the IG trademark removed. They are *not* old. They were made in the mid 1960s.

Aside from the presence of the IG trademark, there are other ways to tell the new pieces from the old. The new glass is thicker, heavier, has a bulkier feel to it, and the molding and pattern detail is often less sharp. The glass was made thicker and heavier to cut down on breakage and loss at the time of manufacture. Also, many of the new pieces have a heavily stippled, textured effect on the underside of the collar base. Thus, when the IG trademark is ground off, a telltale smooth spot clearly shows up against this stippled area.

On December 19, 1972, Imperial became a subsidiary of the Lenox Corporation of New Jersey. They became officially known as IGC Liquidating Corporation. Production of new carnival glass continued and a new trademark was adopted. A capital letter L which, of course, stood for Lenox, was added to the logo.

Imperial Glass Company Trademark
as
IGC Liquidating Corporation
1973 – 1981

Any carnival glass bearing this mark was made between 1973 and 1981. Colors made during this period include amber, green, pink, pastel blue, and amethyst.

In 1981, Imperial was again sold, this time to a private investor, Arthur Lorch, and another new trademark was adopted. Mr. Lorch added a slanted capitol letter A to the mark. Production of new carnival glass continued under Mr. Lorch's ownership.

Imperial Glass Company Trademark
under
Arthur Lorch Ownership
1981 – 1982

Any Imperial carnival glass bearing this mark was made during 1981 and 1982.

After little more than a year under the ownership of Arthur Lorch, Imperial changed hands again for the final time. Mr. Robert Stahl acquired the company in late 1982. Reportedly, the company was going to adopt a trademark consisting of a capitol letter N superimposed over a capital letter I, to stand for New Imperial. It has been reported that some pieces of new carnival were made with this trademark. If so, they were made in extremely small quantities. I have never seen any new carnival with this mark.

In 1984 Mr. Stahl declared bankruptcy. The Imperial factory closed its doors on April 11, 1985. Most of the assets, including all of the Imperial, Heisey, and Cambridge molds, were sold at auction or privately. They were, in effect, "scattered to the winds" among several glass collectors' societies and several other glass manufacturers. Some of this dispersal was as follows:

The Heisey Collectors of America purchased virtually all of the some 3,000 Heisey molds owned by Imperial. They are now stored and displayed in the Heisey Museum.

The Cambridge Glass Collectors of America purchased many, though not all, of the Cambridge molds owned by Imperial.

The National Imperial Glass Collectors Society Inc. purchased several of the original Imperial molds, including the mold for the Robin mug.

Most of the remaining Imperial molds are now in the hands of several other glass companies. Some of these are as follows:

WETZEL GLASS — Owns several Imperial molds, including some in Imperial's Grape, Lustre Rose, and others.

SUMMIT ART GLASS — Owns several molds in Windmill, Fashion, Lustre Rose, and, among others, the mold for the Homestead plate.

Other Imperial molds were purchased by Mirror Images and The Boyd/Crystal Art Glass Company.

Summit Art Glass has reproduced new carnival items in many of the patterns that they own that are listed above. Colors made include red, pink, blue, and yellow. Most of them are marked with their capitol S logo.

With the dispersal of Imperial's molds, future reproductions of Imperial carnival patterns are virtually assured. Fortunately, most of those made thusfar are in colors not originally made by Imperial. My best advice to the wise collector is to do what I do. If you are willing to invest the time, money, and effort in collecting old carnival glass, then invest some time and effort in learning about new carnival glass as well. Seek out the gift shops and stores that sell new glassware. See what is being made and keep yourself up to date. It pays.

The following four pages are reprinted from Imperial factory catalogs, circa 1971 – 1972. They are presented here to give the collector a perspective on some of the new carnival glass that Imperial produced. These pages offer New Imperial carnival in marigold, smoke, white, and red. Many of these same pieces were later offered in green, blue, amber, ice blue, pink, and amethyst. Learn to recognize them and the trademarks that Imperial used between 1962 and 1984, and you will have no trouble in telling the old Imperial carnival glass from the new.

# CARNIVAL GLASS (ALL ITEMS AVAILABLE IN RUBIGOLD OR PEACOCK)

678
oz. Tumbler

678
3 Pint Pitcher/Vase

489
9 oz. Tumbler
Rose

24
3 Pint Pitcher/Vase
Rose

473
10 oz.
Tumbler
Grape

473
3 Pint Pitcher/Vase
Grape

*514/S
9 oz.
Tumbler

*239/S
3 Pint Pitcher

*Sueded Rubigold Only

473
1 Pint Pitcher/Vase
Grape

525
10-1/2" Plate
"Homestead"

62D
10-1/2" Plate
Rose

176
4-Toed
Jar and Cover

619
Box and Cover
Zodiac

282
Covered Jar

282/1
Jar and Cover

975
Box and Cover

475/2
Covered Box

149
Turkey-on-Nest

425
Footed Jar
and Cover

500
15 Piece Punch Set

33

CARNIVAL GLASS

356 – 10" Vase
Loganberry

287 – 10" Vase
Grape

40 – 9-1/2"
Tall Basket

181 – 6-1/4" Vase
Rose

536
6" Vase

529
10" Vase

480
9-1/2" Vase

9C
1/4" Crimped
Nappy, Grape

212
4-1/2" Compote

505A
7-3/4" Tall Compote

1590/45
5-1/2" Compote
Zodiac

474C
6" Footed Compote

473
10 oz. Goblet
Grape

163
Decanter
& Stopper
Grape

473
3 oz. Wine
Grape

505
Toothpick
Holder

831
Footed Sugar and Cream Set
Grape

630
Bell, Hobnail

1886/350
Oil Lamp

96
Salt and Pepper Se
Grape

161
Butter and Cover, Rose

2526
Sugar and Cream Set, Rose

478
5-1/2" Handled
Nappy, Pansy

400
8" Swan

47C
9" Crimped Bowl, Grape

880
3-1/2" Candleholder
Grape

737A
8-1/2" Footed
Bowl

160
3-1/2" Candleholder
Rose

113C
11-1/2" 3-Toed
Crimped Bowl
Rose

858   6" Handled  Pickle Tray, Grape

49
4-1/2" Bowl
Grape

478C 8-1/2"
Crimped Oval Bowl , Pansy

438
8" Bowl

74C
8" 3-Toed
Crimped Bowl
Rose

# WHITE CARNIVAL

524
10-1/2" Plate
"Mum"

525
10-1/2" Plate
"Homestead"

670
Water Tumbler
"Robin"

670
3 Pint
Pitcher
"Robin"

473
1 Pint
Pitcher
Grape

356
10" Vase
Loganberry

489
7-1/2" 3-Toed
Bowl, Rose

160
3-1/2" Candleholder
Rose

62C
9" Crimped
Bowl, Rose

1155
4-1/2" Candleholder

1152
10" 3-Toed
Bowl

496
7" Bowl

809
Suzanne
Bell

161
Butter and Cover
Rose

2526
Sugar and Cream Set
Rose

3800/42C
5" Compote

505A
4-3/4" Compote

109
6-1/2" Vase
Loganberry

536
6" Vase

975
Box and Cover

478C
8-1/2" Crimped
Oval Bowl
Pansy

147
4-1/2" Swan

7
Toothpick
Holder

1155N
3" 3-Toed
Nappy

478
5-1/2" Handled
Nappy, Pansy

# SUNSET RUBY
### (CARNIVAL GLASS)

3800/42C
5" Compote

474C
7-1/2" Compote

474
6-1/2" Vase

505
8" Footed Vase

494
9 oz. Tumbler

494
9" Pitcher/Vase

489C
8" Bowl
Rose

434N
7" Bowl

3800/72
3" Candleholder

3800/49B
7" 4-Toed
Bowl

3800/165
Covered Box

975
Box and Cover

3800/165C
7" 3-Toed Compote

5057
8" Bowl

210
"Robin" Mug

1560
Box and Cover

147
4" Swan

3800/27
Sugar and Cream
Set

478
5-1/2" Handled Nappy
Pansy

402
Toothpick Holder

IMPERIAL GLASS CORPORATION, BELLAIRE, OHIO 43906

36

# IMPERIAL'S REPRODUCTION CARNIVAL COLORS

The following is a listing of the colors made by Imperial in their reproduction carnival lines between 1962 and 1981. This listing is by no means complete. It is presented here for the purpose of helping to identify the Imperial reproduction carnival colors. The dates listed are the dates that the particular colors were added to the line. Production of the colors was often continued in varying degrees well after the dates listed.

RUBIGOLD (MARIGOLD) — 1962. A wide variety of shapes and patterns. Production continued in varying degrees for several years.

PEACOCK (SMOKE) — 1965. A wide variety of shapes and patterns.

HELIOS GREEN — 1967. A wide variety of shapes and patterns, but somewhat more limited than others.

RED — 1968. Fieldflower water set, Robin mug, items in Diamond Lace, Lustre Rose, Octagon, Pansy, and items from Cambridge molds. Made again in 1972.

AZURE BLUE (ICE BLUE) — 1969. Several items including the Tiger Lily water set.

AURORA JEWELS (COBALT) — 1970. Windmill pieces and several items from Cambridge molds.

WHITE — 1972. Items in Lustre Rose, Hattie, Pansy, Robin water set, Homestead plate, Chrysanthemum plate, and items from Cabridge molds.

AMBER — 1973. Several items including a line of commemorative plates in the America series.

MEADOW GREEN (EMERALD) — 1978. Items in Lustre Rose, Three in One, and several others.

PINK — 1978. Items in Lustre Rose, Four Seventy Four, and others. Production continued through 1981.

HORIZON BLUE — 1979. Just slightly darker than ice blue. One of the last colors developed at Imperial. Items made include the Robin water set.

AMETHYST — 1981. Twenty-one items in the line. One of the last regular production runs of new carnival at Imperial.

Imperial also produced several other new carnival colors on a limited edition basis for special order customers. From 1973 to 1976, they produced a special edition of carnival shapes and colors for the American Bicentennial, including the Liberty Bell line. Many commemorative and souvenir pieces were also made for the International Carnival Glass Association and the American Carnival Glass Association.

# NOT IMPERIAL

Over the years, we, as carnival glass collectors, have gotten into a very bad habit. For some reason we automatically assume that every geometric design that is found primarily in marigold and is of unknown origin must be an Imperial product. As a result, Imperial has been credited with producing a number of patterns that, in reality, never saw the inside of the Imperial factory. It is now time to correct some of these mis-attributions.

You will not find any of the following patterns illustrated in the book. They have all been credited to Imperial. However, recent findings by this writer and many other knowledgeable researchers have proven them to be products of other firms, or have, at the very least, cast serious doubt on an Imperial attribution.

HOBSTAR BAND — Known in two styles of water sets, a handled celery vase, and a large, stemmed compote, reported only in marigold. A growing body of evidence now points towards the U.S. Glass Company (or possibly even the Indiana Glass Company) as the maker. The pattern does not appear in any of the known Imperial factory catalogs. While beautifully iridized examples do exist, many are found with a very pale, washed-out iridescence which is not typical of Imperial. It is, however, typical of several marigold items from U.S. Glass Company. The design more closely resembles several other patterns made by U.S. Glass. Also, the water pitcher is strikingly similar to a pattern called Nogi which was a product of the Indiana Glass Company. This Nogi pattern, made in non-iridized crystal, was produced in two styles of water sets. Both are virtually identical in configuration to the two styles of Hobstar Band water sets.

DIAMOND & FILE — Found primarily in rather small bowls and vases of varying heights, in marigold. This is now known to be a Fenton product. It appears in company with other known Fenton designs in several different issues of Butler Brothers Wholesale Catalogs.

DIAMOND POINT COLUMNS — Most often seen in creamers, small, covered powder jars, and berry sets, only in marigold. The design does not appear in any of the Imperial Factory catalogs, and the quality of the glass itself, which is modest at best, is not typical of Imperial. The pattern does not appear in the wholesale catalogs until the mid 1920. Recent evidence now suggests this design may be a product of either Hazel Atlas or Hocking.

DIAMOND FLUTE — This pattern is definitely a product of the U.S. Glass Company and dates from the late 1920s. It was made in an extensive variety of iridized and non-iridized shapes. Depression glass collectors know this pattern as Aunt Polly.

DIAMOND FOUNTAIN — Known only in a cruet, in marigold, this design is now known to be a product of the Higbee Glass Company.

STORK ABC — Known only in a child's dish, in marigold. More research is needed here, but it is starting to look like this is a U.S. Glass Company product.

NUMBER 4 — For many years, this design has been listed in virtually all carnival reference sources as Imperial's #4. This pattern is not an Imperial product. It was made by the Jeannette Glass Company, and the original pattern name is Anniversary. It was produced in both iridized and non-iridized glass from 1947 through the mid-1960s, far too late, in this writer's opinion, to even be classified as old carnival glass! The most often seen shape is a small, 5" – 6" footed bowl, usually found in a rather pale, washed-out shade of marigold. A full line of plates, cups, saucers, and various serving pieces was made.

STUDS — Best know in a juice set. Consisting of a small pitcher, dome-footed juice glasses, and a round serving tray, this pattern is also a product of the Jeannette Glass Company. The original pattern name is Holiday, and it was produced from 1947 through the mid-1950s. Here again, this is far too late to be classified as old carnival glass.

GOLDEN HONEYCOMB — This pattern is a product of the Jeannette Glass Company. The original pattern name is Hex Optic. The non-iridized pieces date from the mid 1930s, while the marigold iridescent pieces were made very late, circa 1950.

# IMPERIAL'S CARNIVAL GLASS PATTERNS, SHAPES, AND COLORS

All of Imperial's carnival glass patterns are presented here in alphabetical order. All of the shapes and colors known for each pattern are listed. This information was compiled from the author's research and from reports from collectors all around the country. Every effort has been made to insure the accuracy of the information presented here. Of course, no one person can know it all, and it is likely that some shapes and colors have been missed. New finds, colors, and shapes are constantly surfacing. Even after nearly 30 years of active carnival glass collecting, we still make new discoveries. At least five or six previously unreported Imperial carnival pieces turned up during the writing of this book!

A few notes regarding color classifications should be mentioned here. One of the most important is in regard to the colors known as helios, green, and emerald. An important distinction between the three colors must be made. They are a world apart in color, desirability, rarity, and value. A quick review of these three colors is in order.

HELIOS — A light to medium green with a silver/gold iridescent sheen. There is little, if any, multicolor iridescent highlights. This color was produced on a large scale and is not a particular favorite with many collectors. The value and desirability factors for many pieces in this color are not that high.

GREEN — A medium shade of green with a satin, metallic iridescence. Good multicolor highlights are present, with a strong gold tone predominating.

EMERALD — A rich, deep emerald green with a brilliant, multicolor, iridescence which often rivals the iridescent lustre found on Imperial's purple carnival. Very little of it was produced and examples in most patterns are *extremely* rare.

Also, the color listed in this book as purple includes the color called amethyst. At the time of manufacture, both were intended to be the same color. Minor variations in temperature and chemical mix created variations in color shade when a batch of glass was made.

One of the relatively few stylized, naturalistic patterns made by Imperial, Acanthus is listed in the old factory catalogs as Imperial's #465. It first appeared in the wholesale catalogs in the spring of 1911. Only two shapes are known, 8" – 9" bowls, which may be ruffled or of a deep, round shape and a true, flat plate. The plates are in the 10" size range, which qualifies them as chop plates.

The bowls are most often found in marigold, followed by clambroth, smoke, and purple, in that order. Helios examples are much harder to find and aqua ones are very rare. Extremely rare bowls in emerald and cobalt blue have also been reported.

Plates have only been confirmed in three colors. The most often found in marigold, and they turn up in pretty fair numbers. Smoke examples are much harder to find. By far, the

*Acanthus 9" bowl in purple.*

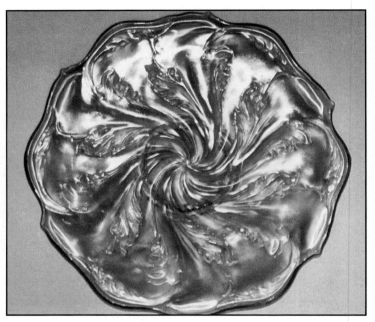

*Acanthus 10" plate in marigold.*

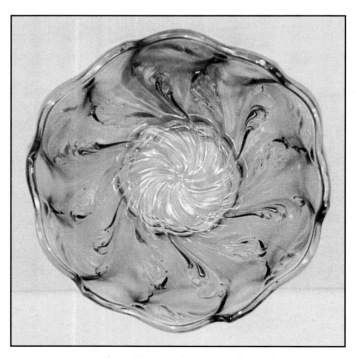

*Acanthus 8" bowl in pastel smoke.*

rarest of the plates are the clambroth examples. In 26 years of collecting, I have seen exactly two. Surely others must exist. No plates have yet surfaced in purple, helios, emerald, cobalt blue, or aqua, but they could well turn up. Be on the lookout for them.

**Shapes and Colors Known**

Bowl, 8" – 9" — marigold, purple, smoke, helios, emerald, aqua, clambroth, cobalt blue
Plate, 10" — marigold, smoke, clambroth

## Arcs

This design dates from the 1910 period when it first appeared in the wholesale catalogs. It is found primarily as an exterior pattern often combined with Pansy, Cobblestones, and Star of David, as interior designs.

Because of its use as an exterior design, it can be found in all of the colors known in its interior design companions. I cannot recall ever seeing an example of Arcs without an accompanying interior pattern.

**Shapes and Colors Known**

Bowls, 8" – 9", exterior only — marigold, purple, helios, smoke, clambroth, amber, emerald, blue (possibly others)

*Arcs*

## Balloons

This is one of the very few entirely hand-blown and hand-cut carnival designs made by Imperial. The balloon design is hand-cut onto a delicate, thin, blown glass. Because of their delicacy, relatively few examples have survived the years.

Vases, in four sizes and three shape variations, are the most often seen examples. The most easily found of these is a squat, ovoid shape, standing 6½" tall. Two sizes of corset-shaped vases, standing 7½" and 9½" tall are also known, but are found far less often. The other vase

41

shape is a straight-sided beaker shape, 9" tall. All four shapes have been reported only in marigold and smoke, with marigold the most often found.

The pattern may also be found on an 11" – 12" center-handled server. This item is not blown, but pressed. Here again, marigold and smoke are the only reported colors. The iridescence on these servers often shows a heavy, onion-skin, stretch effect — something not found on the vases. It is also somewhat more easily found. The edge of the server may be flat, like a plate, or turned up. The center handle has a flat top and is rather square-like in appearance.

The only other reported shapes are a delicate, blown, stemmed compote and a very pretty little perfume atomizer. Both are known only in marigold.

*Balloons*

## Shapes and Colors Known

Vases, 6½" – 9½", four shapes — marigold, smoke
Center-handled server — marigold, smoke
Compote — marigold
Perfume Atomizer — marigold

## Banded Ribs

This design is included here as a possible Imperial creation. While the quality of the iridescence is certainly typical of Imperial, we have no concrete evidence to place it in the Imperial family. The design does not appear in any of the existing Imperial factory catalogs, nor does it appear in any of the Imperial carnival assortments in any of the wholesale catalogs. The pattern is suspiciously similar to Hocking's Optic Block design which was produced from 1929 to 1935. Perhaps future research will provide a conclusive attribution. Until then, it is presented here with considerable reservations.

Banded Ribs is known only in water sets, the style of which are consistent with those of the Depression years. The only color reported is a good, rich marigold, usually with an outstanding radium lustre.

***Banded Ribs*** *water pitcher and tumbler in marigold.*

**Shapes and Colors Known**

Water pitcher and tumbler — marigold

## Beaded Acanthus

In the introduction to this book, I wrote that Imperial produced an extensive array of functional, utilitarian pieces, more than any of their competitors. Milk pitchers certainly fall into this category and Imperial produced more of them than any of the other carnival glass producing firms. Beaded Acanthus is one of the designs that was used exclusively for this shape. This was Imperial's #78 pattern, and it appeared in the non-iridized crystal in the very first Imperial factory catalog, issued in 1904.

***Beaded Acanthus*** *milk pitcher in marigold.*
*The only shape known in this design.*

Marigold is the most often found color. Even so, these pitchers seem to be a little harder to come by then many of the other Imperial milk pitchers. Still, they are available, with a little persistent searching. Very rare examples in smoke are also known, but are seldom found. For years, rumors have circulated about the existence of emerald examples, but all efforts by this writer to confirm them have proved fruitless. An example in any colors other than marigold and smoke would be a rare find.

**Shapes and Colors Known**

Milk pitcher, 7" — marigold, smoke

## Beaded Bullseye

This design is found only on the exterior surface of vases which may vary in height from 6" to as much as 14". The shape of the vases may also vary considerably. Some are only 6" tall, with the top portion flared out to a nearly equal diameter. Other, taller examples are nearly cylindrical in shape, with the top portion barely flared at all. Most examples are from 8" to 11" tall, with a top flared to a diameter of between 4" to 5½".

Marigold and purple examples are the most often seen, but even these are somewhat scarce. Vases in helios and amber are even harder to find, and the smoke examples are quite rare. A few very rare examples in an unusual shade of pastel lime green have also been reported. The top honors go to the cobalt blue examples. Only a few are known. In fact, it has been 10 years since one of them changed hands at one of the carnival glass auctions.

The quality of the iridescence is outstanding on most of the examples found, in any of the colors. Very few are poorly iridized and they make a handsome addition to any collection.

**Shapes and Colors Known**

Vase, 6" – 14" — marigold, purple, helios, smoke, amber, lime green, cobalt blue, green

***Beaded Bullseye*** *squat vases in purple and marigold. The top of the purple example is flared to a diameter nearly equal to its height.*

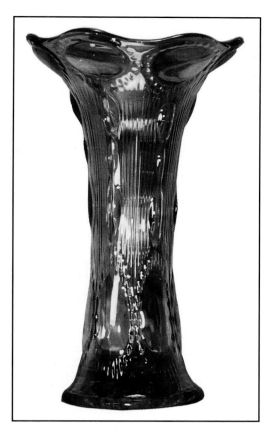

*This beautiful 11" purple **Beaded Bullseye** vase is of the height and shape that is most frequently found.*

*__Beaded Bullseye__ 9" vase in helios. This is actually a rather scarce color for this.*

## Bellaire Souvenir

The Bellaire souvenir bowl remains one of the mysteries of Imperial carnival glass production. These round, 7" bowls have a large bell molded in the center surrounded by the lettering, "Bellaire — Good Will Tour." The exterior carries a Smooth Rib design. To put it in simple terms, we simply don't have a clue regarding the occasion for which these bowls were made. The only color known is marigold and these bowls are quite scarce.

### Shapes and Colors Known

Bellaire souvenir bowl, 7" — marigold

***Bellaire Souvenir***

This pattern appears in the old Imperial factory catalogs with the curious design number of Snap-14. The carnival glass version first appeared in the wholesale catalogs in 1911.

Punch sets are the most well known of the carnival shapes. Most examples of the punch bowl are of a round, deep shape, but a few ruffled examples are also know. Marigold is the color most often seen, but even this is rather scarce and underrated. Purple is the only other color reported. Many of these exhibit something rather unusual for Imperial's purple carnival — a rather dull, silvery, gun-metal-like iridescence. This often detracts from their value. However, examples with a dazzling, multicolor iridescent lustre do exist, and are highly treasured. They will command serious prices when offered for sale.

The only other shapes reported are collar based, ruffled bowls in the 8" – 9" size range. They are found most often in marigold and only rarely in purple.

*Broken Arches* punch set in purple. This example has a plain interior, while some are found with a ribbed interior design.

**Shapes and Colors Known**

Punch bowl and base — marigold, purple
Punch cup — marigold, purple
Bowl, 8" – 9" — marigold, purple

## Chatelaine

Many consider the Chatelaine water set to be near the top of the list in both rarity and beauty. The mold work is flawless and the rich, brilliant, iridescent lustre is often beyond belief. Purple is the only color confirmed, to date, on the these very rare sets. For years, rumors have persisted regarding the existence of marigold tumblers. None have ever been confirmed. Still, most Imperial water sets are known in marigold, so the possibility is always there.

There has also been some uncertainty regarding an Imperial attribution. This uncertainty can now be laid to rest. The Chatelaine water pitcher appears in the mid spring, 1913, Butler

Brothers Wholesale Catalog, in company with other confirmed Imperial patterns.

While many of Imperial's geometric patterns can be found in a variety of shapes, Chatelaine is known only in a water set. They are highly treasured by collectors and seldom change hands.

**Shapes and Colors Known**

Water pitcher, tumbler — purple

*Chatelaine Water Pitcher and Tumbler in purple. This is one of the rarest and most desirable of Imperial's carnival water set designs.*

## Chesterfield #600

In the earlier Imperial factory catalogs this design appears simply designated as Imperial's #600 line. Later catalogs illustrate it as the Chesterfield pattern. Many of the items in this line have, in the past, been erroneously called Flute Variants. Some have also been called Colonial and Wide Panel. If we can get used to using the name Chesterfield, much of the confusion surrounding all of these very similar designs will no longer exist.

Many of the pieces in the Chesterfield line are handled, and herein lies an easy way to distinguish them from the Flute #700 and Colonial #593 lines. The handles on the Chesterfield are flat at the top portion, while the handles on the Flute and Colonial pieces come to a distinct point at the top.

Perhaps the most familiar item in this line is the pedestal based, handled lemonade mug. It is known only in marigold. Some collectors have called this mug "The Chesterfield Tumbler," but this is incorrect. There *is* a true, proper Chesterfield tumbler, and it is *not* handled. This mug should rightfully be called the Chesterfield lemonade mug.

The Chesterfield water pitcher is a tall, straight-sided tankard pitcher. The shape of the handle is identical to that of the Chesterfield mug. This pitcher came with a cover, but most of these covers seem to have become casualties of time and use. They are rarely found today. The matching tumbler stands 5" tall and has, in the past, been labeled Colonial or Colonial Stretch. This is the true Chesterfield tumbler. It is shown, with the pitcher that is described above, in the old Imperial factory catalogs. Both the pitcher and tumblers are known in marigold, white, teal, celeste blue, and red, often showing a stretch effect to the iridescence.

Another item in this Chesterfield line is the handled toothpick holder. This has been in the past, incorrectly called the Flute Variant toothpick holder. The handles are of the same configuration described for the mug and the water pitcher, and it is listed in the Imperial factory catalog with the same #600 designation. All of them have, in the past, been mistakenly called Flute, Colonial, or Wide Panel. The large, 11" compote, illustrated here in red, has been called Wide Panel. It is not. It appears in the catalog with the #600 designation, and is part of the Chesterfield line. This compote is also known in marigold, clambroth, white, teal, and celeste blue, all often found with stretch iridescence. A smaller, 5" – 6" diameter version is also known in the same colors. Stemmed sherbets, known in the exact same aforementioned colors, have also been mistakenly called Flute or Colonial. A tiny, pedestal-based open salt is also part of the Chesterfield #600 line. It is known only in marigold. The only other shapes with this designation number are candlesticks, hexagonal in shape, and resting on a hexagonal, domed foot. These are known in marigold, smoke, and clambroth.

*Chesterfield #600 tumblers in white, red, and celeste blue. In the past, these have been incorrectly called Colonial Stretch.*

*The marigold Chesterfield mug.*

*This tiny marigold Chesterfield open table salt is signed with the Imperial Cross Mark.*

*Once called Wide Panel, Imperial factory catalogs prove that this compote, shown here in red, is actually part of the Chesterfield #600 line.*

I realize that this is a tremendous amount of change to swallow; however, the old Imperial factory catalog designation numbers don't lie. I do not fault earlier carnival glass researchers for mistakenly labeling many of these items as Colonial, Flute, or Wide Panel. You must realize that in the early days of carnival glass collecting, we did not have the resources and information at our disposal that we do now. As new information and resources become available, change and re-thinking is inevitable. If you think about it a moment, using the name Chesterfield for all of the above described pieces will virtually eliminate all of the confusion surrounding the various Flute, Colonial, and Wide Panel-type designs. It will take a little getting used to, but in the long run it will make things a lot easier.

*A very scarce **Chesterfield** rose bowl in smoke.*

## Shapes and Colors Known

Candlesticks — marigold, clambroth, smoke
Compote, small 5" – 6" — marigold, clambroth, smoke, celeste blue, white, red, teal
Lemonade mug — marigold
Open salt — marigold
Sherbet, stemmed — marigold, clambroth, smoke, celeste blue, white, red, teal
Tankard pitcher, covered — marigold, white, red, celeste, blue, teal
Tumbler, 5" — marigold, white, red, celeste blue, teal
Toothpick holder, handled — marigold
Rose bowl, collar base — marigold, smoke, clambroth
Stemmed rose bowl — marigold, clambroth, white

## Chrysanthemum

This pattern obviously entered production at the same time as its close cousin, Homestead. Chrysanthemum, like Homestead, is found only on the interior of 10½" chop plates with a ribbed exterior. Some examples are trademarked NUART, and some are not. This trademark will be found in the lower right portion of the interior surface. These plates are not known in quite as many colors as the Homestead plate, and are generally even harder to find. The quality of the mold work and the caliber of the iridescence makes these plates highly treasured and much sought additions to any collection.

Marigold and purple examples are the most available, but even they are really quite rare. Amber and smoke examples are much harder still to come by, and the white examples are even rarer. The helios plates are rare, with only about eight or ten examples reported. Some of these almost border on emerald, showing a rich multicolor lustre. The cobalt blue examples top the rarity list with only two or three reported. A Chrysanthemum chop plate in *any* color is really a rare find today.

***Chrysanthemum.*** *The Imperial NUART trademark can be clearly seen in the lower right-hand corner of this beautiful amber plate. The equally magnificent purple example is unsigned.*

These plates were reproduced in the 1960s and 1970s. The new plates have a plain exterior and are marked with the IG trademark. Colors made include marigold, smoke, amber, white, and helios.

### Shapes and Colors Known

Chop plate, 10½" — Marigold, purple, helios, amber, white, smoke, cobalt blue

## Cobblestones

A most unusual design, as Imperial patterns go, Cobblestones is most often found in 8½" to 9½" ruffled bowls. The exterior carries the Imperial's Arcs pattern. It is a rather tough pattern to find, and examples are not often encountered in any color. Apparently the design's production run was a relatively short one.

Most Imperial carnival is easily found in marigold and very scarce to very rare in purple. Here, the situation is reversed. Purple Cobblestones bowls are by far the most frequently seen. A reasonable number of helios examples also turn up. The marigold bowls are actually quite scarce. In fact, only a couple of marigold examples have changed hands at the carnival glass auctions in the last ten years. This bowl may also be found in amber, and these are rarely seen. By far the rarest is the cobalt blue Cobblestones bowl. Only a couple of them are known.

An extremely rare 9" flat plate also exists. Only one example, in purple, is known.

*Cobblestones* 9" *ruffled bowl in purple. The exterior carries the Arcs pattern.*

**Shapes and Colors Known**

Bowl, ruffled, 8½" – 9½" — marigold, purple, helios, amber, cobalt blue
Plate, 9" — purple

## Colonial

Colonial is one of four designs in this book that have caused a great deal of confusion. Over the years, collectors have gotten items in the Colonial, Flute, Wide Panel, and Chesterfield patterns almost hopelessly mixed up. All of these designs appear in the old Imperial factory catalogs, each with their own individual pattern numbers. So with the aid of these catalogs, we can finally begin to sort it all out. (NOTE: If you first read the sections in this book on Flute, Chesterfield, and Wide Panel, the whole mess becomes clear.)

Only four items in the old Imperial factory catalogs can rightfully be called Colonial. They bear the designations of Imperial's #593 design, and in the case of the candlesticks, Imperial's #41 designation. We have no choice other than to call them Colonial.

The Colonial lemonade mug is easily distinguished from the Chesterfield mug. The Colonial mug rests on an octagonal base and the top of the handle curves upward to a distinct point. It is known only in marigold, and is a little on the scarce side.

The Colonial buttermilk goblet is likewise known only in marigold, and has often been mistakenly called Flute on Wide Panel. These are, perhaps, the most easily found of all carnival glass goblets, so they must have been a popular seller.

The Colonial candlesticks are octagonal in shape. They are found in 7" and 9" tall sizes. The are easily found in marigold and clambroth. Rare examples in purple and amber are also known.

Rounding out the Colonial shapes known are the small, straight-sided breakfast creamer and open sugar. They are known only in marigold.

*Colonial* buttermilk goblets and breakfast sugar and creamer in marigold.

**Shapes and Colors Known**

Buttermilk goblet — marigold
Lemonade mug — marigold
Candlesticks, 7" or 9" — marigold, clambroth, purple, amber
Breakfast creamer and sugar — marigold

## Colonial Lady

It has always been my belief that patterns should never be given names based solely on shape. That's asking for trouble. Whenever this is done, inevitably, a previously undocumented shape surfaces. The pattern name then becomes meaningless, and confusion is often the result. The case of the Colonial Lady vase is a classic example.

These rare and beautiful vases were named many years ago, based primarily on their unique corset shape. While this book was in preparation, I received the photograph of the previously unlisted marigold example that is shown here. As you can clearly see, it is completely different in shape. So much so, that the owners did not recognize it as the Colonial Lady pattern. I must confess that it took me a few moments, along with a careful comparison with one of the usual Colonial Lady shapes, to realize that this vase was indeed a Colonial Lady. I can't help wondering how many other collectors have viewed this rare vase and never made the connection. It would come as no surprise that other, similarly (or even differently) shaped examples sit innocently in other collections, the owners unaware of what they have, all because the pattern was given a name based solely on shape.

Regardless of shape, anyone who doubts the quality of the iridescence that Imperial was capable of has certainly never seen one of these little jewels. They bring raves whenever they are shown. The iridescence on most examples simply defies description.

The corset-shaped examples stand from 5½" to 6" tall. The shaping of the top may vary slightly, but the purple example shown here with a pinched, somewhat square ruffle, is the style usually found. This is one of the few Imperial pieces that is most frequently found in a deep, rich purple. Even so, they are rarely encountered and highly treasured. Marigold examples do exist, but are extremely rare. Only a relatively few are known. In fact, only one marigold corset-shaped example has sold, at auction, in the last ten years. No other colors in this shape have been reported.

The other shape variation, shown here for the first time, has been reported only in marigold. It stands 8⅜" tall and has eight ruffles and a top diameter of 6¼". In fact, the example shown here is the only known example, to date, in any color. I would not be surprised if others exist in purple.

*Standard corset-shaped **Colonial Lady** vases in marigold and purple. The marigold examples are far more rare than the purple.*

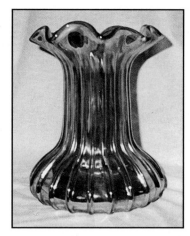

*The marigold **Colonial Lady** shape variation that is shown here, for the first time, is 8" tall.*

**Shapes and Colors Known**

Vase, corset shaped — marigold, purple
Vase, bulbous base, flared, ruffled top, 8⅜" — marigold

## Columbia

Here is a classic case of getting the most mileage out of a set of molds. Of the five known carnival shapes, four were fashioned from the same mold. Imperial factory catalogs list this design as Imperial's #246.

Carnival shapes known include vases, bowls, rose bowls, and a flat plate, all made from the same basic mold. The stemmed compote was made from a separate mold. All of these are most often seen in marigold. The vases and the compotes are the most abundant shapes, the bowls are scarce, and the plate is rare. The rose bowl is extremely rare, with only a couple of examples known.

Other colors do exist and the situation regarding them is very different. Vases have been reported in smoke, helios, and purple. All are rare, with the purple examples extremely so. While they may not realize equal value, the ruffled compote is also extremely rare in purple. The flattened plates, which may range in size from 7½" to 9", have been reported in clambroth, but no other colors have yet been confirmed. The iridescence on all shapes is usually of a stunning quality.

These five shapes are the only carnival ones to be confirmed, but others are definitely possible. An old Imperial factory catalog illustrates no less that 16 shapes in non-iridized crystal. These include many size and shape variations in vases, compotes, bowls, and plates. So be on the lookout for them. You might just find a one-of-a-kind sleeper.

*The extremely rare marigold **Columbia** rose bowl.*

*The clambroth **Columbia** whimsey plate is quite scarce. The marigold vase is the most often seen of the shapes in this pattern. The marigold compote is also scarce.*

**Shapes and Colors Known**

Vase, 5" – 7" — marigold, purple, helios, smoke
Compote, ruffled — marigold, purple
Plate, 7½" – 9" — marigold, clambroth
Bowl, 7" – 8" — marigold
Rose bowl — marigold

## Cone & Tie

A great deal of mystery surrounds this pattern and it is presented here only as a likely Imperial design. Its only appearance in the wholesale catalogs occurs in a spring 1908 issue in non-iridized crystal. It is part of an assortment of four different tumblers. As of this writing, we cannot assign a specific maker to any of the other three tumblers, so the origins of Cone & Tie remain speculative. Based on color and iridescent quality, an Imperial attribution does seem likely.

Very rare tumblers are the only shapes known. All of the known examples are in deep, rich purple and the quality of the iridescence is superb. No matching water pitcher has ever surfaced, which only adds to the mystery. If one were to be found, it would, of course, be a rarity of the highest possible order. Since 1983, only two examples of the tumbler have changed hands at the carnival glass auctions.

*Cone & Tie tumbler in purple, the only color in which this design is known. No matching water pitchers have ever been found.*

**Shapes and Colors Known**

Tumbler — purple

## Corn Bottle

Standing just 5" tall, these unusual little bottles were likely made as a premium item for a specific customer. They do not appear in any of the known wholesale catalogs of the period, a fact that tends to confirm this theory. They are often found with a cork stopper. There has been a great deal of speculation as to what they contained, ranging from corn syrup to some form of liquor. Personally, I feel that the latter is the most likely. The Imperial attribution is based primarily on the colors in which they are found. Marigold is the most often seen color, with smoke and helios following, in that order; however, the difference in rarity between the three is slight and all are really rather scarce. Some of the helios examples have an aqua tint to them.

*Corn Bottles in smoke, marigold, and helios.*

In recent years, a number of these bottles have surfaced with silver-plated, metal shaker tops grouted on to them. There is no evidence to suggest that they were originally made that way at the Imperial factory; however, Imperial was known to have sold quantities of glass to several metal-working firms. It is therefore quite possible, and even likely, that one of these firms may have purchased a quantity of these bottles, added the shaker tops, and then marketed them as shakers.

The fact that these bottles never appear in any of the known wholesale catalogs suggests that they were produced strictly for the aforementioned purposes, and were not standard production items for market to the general retail trade.

**Shapes and Colors Known**

Bottle, 5" — marigold, smoke, helios

## Crabclaw

One of the many geometric or near cut type patterns that were produced by Imperial, Crabclaw is best known in water sets. These sets are known only in a good, rich marigold, usually with an impressive, multicolor iridescence. The set would be a real knock-out in purple, but none have ever been reported. Unlike most Imperial carnival tumblers, the Crabclaw tumbler lacks a collar base. It rests on a ground bottom. While not classified as rare, the Crabclaw water set is not all that plentiful, either. It will take some patient searching to come up with one.

*The impressive marigold Crabclaw water pitcher and tumbler.*

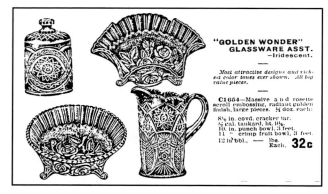

*The Crabclaw water pitcher is feathered in this assortment from the April 1912 Butler Brothers Wholesale Catalog at 32¢ each!*

Crabclaw is also found on berry sets in a wider range of colors. Large and small bowls, usually ruffled, are known in marigold, helios, and purple. Marigold is the most often seen, but a pretty fair number of helios examples also turn up. As with most Imperial patterns, purple examples are rare. The master berry bowl is also known in smoke, but no matching small berry bowls have yet been reported. On the flip side, the small berry bowl has been found in cobalt blue, but no matching master bowl has yet surfaced.

The only other carnival shape confirmed is a rare one indeed. A single example of a cruet, missing the stopper, is known in marigold. It is a rather tall, sharply tapered shape best described as similar to an inverted funnel. While most sources list this item as a cruet, its size suggests that it may have been intended for use as a decanter.

A two-piece fruit bowl and base has been reported in marigold. I cannot help wondering if this is actually a Crabclaw large berry bowl combined with one of the other numerous geometric patterned bases that Imperial is known to have produced. In 26 years of collecting, I have never seen a fruit bowl base with the distinct Crabclaw pattern. I cannot honestly say that I have ever spoken with anyone who has, either. It may well exist, but I cannot, in all conscience, list it here until one is put in front of me. Crabclaw is one Imperial pattern that has not been reproduced.

### Shapes and Colors Known

Water pitcher and tumbler — marigold
Master berry bowl — marigold, purple, helios, smoke
Small berry bowl — marigold, purple, helios, cobalt blue
Cruet (decanter) — marigold
Bowl, ice cream shape — clambroth

## Crackle

I have never been 100% convinced that Crackle is an Imperial pattern. It is included here with considerable reservations. Personally, I lean towards either Jenkins or Jeannette as the likely maker. However, most collectors consider it an Imperial creation, so I shall include it here as a possible Imperial pattern.

Crackle was made in an extensive variety of shapes, all of which are found primarily in marigold. These include bowls, plates, water sets, candlesticks, wall vases, car vases, and covered candy jars. A few of these have been reported in purple and green. Examples in either of those colors are actually very rare, but the popularity of the design just isn't there. As a result, their value levels are very low.

This design came along very late in the carnival era, circa 1930s. Most of the shapes are typical of the glassware of the Depression years. Shapes other than those listed here likely exist.

*Crackle* salt and pepper shakers in marigold on light blue base glass.

### Shapes and Colors Known

Bowls, 5" – 9" — marigold, purple, green
Candy jar, covered — marigold, purple

Candlesticks, two sizes — marigold
Plate, 6" – 8" — marigold, purple, green
Water pitcher and tumbler — Marigold
Wall vase — marigold
Car vase — marigold
Salt and pepper shakers — marigold, marigold on light blue

## Crucifix

Standing 9½" tall, the Crucifix candlestick is the only carnival glass item of a religious nature produced by Imperial. These very rare candlesticks are known only in marigold.

During the last 30 years, they have been reproduced in a wide variety of glass, including carnival. Most of these reproductions were not made by Imperial. These reproductions should really pose no problems to collectors. There are several easy ways to tell the difference between the old carnival candlesticks and the new ones.

The old Crucifix candlestick has a slightly rounded, eight-sided bases. The arms of the cross have rounded edges. The very top of the candleholder is rounded and slightly domed.

The new crucifix candlestick has a squared, six-sided base. The arms of the cross have sharply squared, pointed edges. The top is flared out and has a scalloped effect.

*These marigold* **Crucifix** *candlesticks are quite possibly the rarest of all carnival candlesticks.*

**Shapes and Colors Known**

Candlestick, 9½" — marigold

## Curved Star

A good deal of confusion has surrounded this pattern for many years. It has taken extensive research by many glass researchers to sort it all out. We can now say with a fair degree of confidence that we finally have a pretty clear picture regarding the production of this pattern. It now appears that at least three companies, and possibly four, all made examples of this design.

A wide variety of carnival shapes exist, but we can only credit one of them conclusively to Imperial. The pattern is found on the exterior of some Scroll Embossed compotes. We know that Imperial made this shape, as it appears in some of their early carnival advertising. It is found primarily in a good, rich marigold, but rare purple, helios, and lime green examples have also been reported.

Virtually all of the other shapes in this pattern were made by other firms. The Sowerby Glassworks of Gateshead, England, produced a wide variety of shapes in marigold, blue, and purple carnival. These include butter dishes with the pattern on the inside, compotes, creamers, and bowls. In fact, they produced a Curved Star compote with a Scroll Embossed interior design nearly identical to Imperial's. The Eda Glassworks of Sweden also produced the design in a handsome epergne, a two-piece fruit bowl and base, and a very beautiful chalice. These items are found in marigold and blue.

There is now further evidence that at least two pieces of the Curved Star design may have been made by the U.S. Glass Company. These are a large bowl with an interior design called Headdress, and a version of the covered butter dish. This version of the butter dish has the design on the exterior surface and the base is very flat and plate-like. The configuration is typical of many butter dishes that were made by the U.S. Glass Company.

*Examples of the **Curved Star** pattern in helios and purple. The interior of these compotes carries the Scroll Embossed design. This compote is most often found in marigold.*

**Shapes and Colors Known**
(IMPERIAL ONLY)

Compote, Scroll Embossed interior — marigold, purple, helios, lime green, green

## Daisy

Imperial used this same basic mold and shape for most of their carnival glass baskets. Standing from 9½" to 10½" tall with a diameter of from 5" to 6" at the top of the body, the shape is easily identified by the rope pattern on the handle.

The Daisy basket was apparently one of the later versions of this shape to be made. It does not appear in the wholesale catalogs until the spring of 1929. This probably explains why the number of colors known is so limited. Marigold is the most frequently seen, followed closely by a beautiful, pastel clambroth. The beautiful smoke examples are harder to find. No other colors have been reported.

The Daisy basket is not too difficult to find in any of the colors reported, but be advised that reproductions made in the 1960s and 1970s are also plentiful. New examples in marigold, smoke, and green have the superimposed IG trademark in the base.

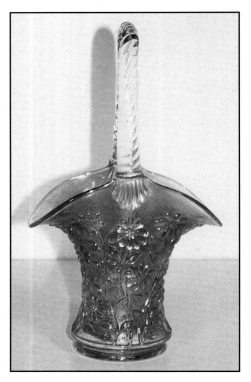

*The **Daisy** basket, in marigold, is one of the more easily found Imperial baskets.*

**Shapes and Colors Known**

Handled basket — marigold, smoke, clambroth

## Diamond Block

Originally called Mount Vernon in the old Imperial factory catalogs, Diamond Block was Imperial's #699 pattern. It seems to have come along rather late in the carnival era. Thirty-four different shapes were produced in non-iridized crystal. The number of shapes reported in carnival is far more limited.

The only colors reported for all shapes, with the exception of the pedestal-footed vase, are marigold and clambroth. Often the color and iridization is rather light, but some examples with a dark, rich marigold lustre are found. The vase has been confirmed in smoke. Most carnival examples of this design are really quite scarce, but they don't seem to command a great deal of attention.

During the preparation of this book, a previously unreported shape surfaced. A large, 12" tall, cylindrical, beaker-shaped vase in marigold was found. It is shown here for the first time.

Carnival shapes other than those listed here likely exist.

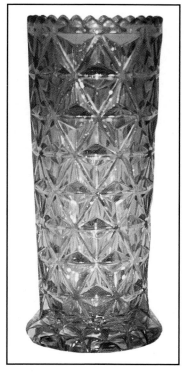

*Diamond Block compote in clambroth.*

*This previously unlisted **Diamond Block** 12" tall, cylindrical vase surfaced while this book was being written.*

### Shapes and Colors Known

Milk pitcher — marigold, clambroth
Tumbler, juice size — marigold, clambroth
Rose bowl — marigold, clambroth
Candlesticks, 9" — marigold, clambroth
Compote — marigold, clambroth
Vase, pedestal-footed, 8" – 9" — Marigold, clambroth, smoke
Vase, cylindrical, 12" — marigold

## Diamond Lace

For years, there was a good deal of controversy concerning the origin of this pattern. This all stemmed from a misattribution to Heisey that was made by Minnie Watson Kamm in her early series of pattern glass books, written way back in the 1940s. To this day, many people still believe the design to be a Heisey product. We now know that, in fact, Heisey produced no iridescent glass. Granted, signed, iridized Heisey pieces do exist, but they were not iridized at the Heisey factory. Heisey sold large quantities of non-iridized crystal to several different decorating firms who, in turn, iridized them using a cold-flashed method. Diamond Lace definitely appears in Imperial factory catalogs with the designation of Imperial's #434½.

The only carnival shapes known are a handsome water set, an equally attractive berry set, and a very rare whimsey rose bowl. A unique situation exists with regard to the water set. It is the only Imperial carnival water set that is commonly found in purple. In fact, purple is the only color in which the pitcher is known. The iridescence on these often defies description. They are absolutely stunning. Fortunately, these purple water sets are reasonably plentiful, giving the collector the opportunity to own an example of Imperial's beautiful purple carnival at a fairly affordable price. However, they are getting more scarce all the time. If you have a chance to buy one, I would do so. A few very rare tumblers are known in marigold, and they bring impressive prices on the rare occasion when they change hands. To date, no marigold water pitchers have been found.

The berry set, comprised of a master 8" – 9" bowl and six small 5" bowls is also known only in marigold and purple. The large master bowls in marigold are quite plentiful, but the small bowls seem to be rather scarce. The purple examples are harder to find, but still turn up from time to time.

The little whimsey rose bowl is extremely rare and known only in marigold. In fact, the example shown here is the only one reported to date. It appears that it may have been shaped from the tumbler mold.

A fairly large, 7" – 8" collar-based rose bowl was reproduced in the 1960s and early 1970s. These are known in red and green, but others may also be possible. They are clearly marked with the IG trademark. No old, large, collar-based rose bowls have been reported, but they could well exist. Imperial often made rose bowls from their 8" – 9" bowl molds.

*No other carnival glass manufacturer could duplicate the magnificent iridescent lustre that Imperial produced on their purple carnival glass. This **Diamond Lace** pitcher is typical of Imperial's purple carnival glass.*

*This little **Diamond Lace** whimsey rose bowl was shaped from the tumbler mold. It is the only one known.*

**Shapes and Colors Known**

Water pitcher — purple
Tumbler — purple, marigold
Berry bowl, 8" – 9" — marigold
Berry bowl, 5" — marigold, purple
Whimsey rose bowl — marigold

# Diamond Ring

Diamond Ring is listed in the early Imperial factory catalogs as Imperial's #88. While the number of shapes made in this design is very limited, the quantity of those shapes produced was apparently quite extensive. Examples are quite easily found.

The most frequently found shapes are 8" – 9" ruffled bowls. Surprisingly, smoke is the most often seen color, but a pretty fair number of marigold examples also turn up. They are also known in purple, but only on rare occasion are they found in that color. Rarest of all are the helios examples — only a few are known. Together with the small 5" – 6" bowls, they make up a most attractive berry set. The small bowls are actually much harder to find, and turn up most often in marigold. Smoke examples are scarce and, here again, purple is rarely found. The helios examples are few and far between.

The only other carnival shape reported is a large rose bowl that was shaped from the same mold as the 8" – 9" ruffled bowl. They have been reported in marigold, purple, and smoke. They are very rare in any color, and are found most often in marigold. Only a few of those are known.

*Relatively few of these **Diamond Ring** rose bowls, in any color, are known.*

## Shapes and Colors Known

Bowl, 8" – 9" — marigold, purple, smoke helios
Bowl, 5" – 6" — marigold, purple, smoke helios
Rose bowl — marigold, purple, smoke

# Diamond and Sunburst

There has been some controversy over the origins of this pattern. Some collectors are convinced that it is a U.S. Glass Company pattern. That firm did make a non-iridized design called Diamond and Sunburst, but it is quite different from the carnival glass pattern that we are dealing with here. On the U.S. Glass version, the central diamond figure is enclosed by interlocking bands of tiny diamonds and the fan-like sunburst designs are much larger. The carnival glass Diamond and Sunburst pattern is definitely an Imperial creation.

Diamond and Sunburst is best known as a design found on wine sets. The decanter and stopper are very similar in configuration to the well-known Imperial's Octagon wine decanter.

The tiny, stemmed wines are slightly smaller than their Octagon cousins. Unlike the Octagon wine set, Diamond and Sunburst wine sets are quite hard to find, even in marigold, and the purple examples are downright rare. Examples in either color usually exhibit exceptionally rich iridescence.

Larger, stemmed goblets have also been reported in marigold only. They are seldom seen.

These are the only shapes that we can credit to Imperial with any degree of confidence. Ruffled bowls have been reported, but virtually every one of these that has been shown to this writer turned out to be examples of Pillow and Sunburst, a similar design that was made by Westmoreland. A large, unusually configured cruet with an applied, scrolled handle is also known, but its design characteristics are not consistent with Imperial Glass. It is very likely of European manufacture.

With a little patience, the **Diamond and Sunburst** wine set can be found in marigold. The magnificent purple sets, like the one shown here, are very rare.

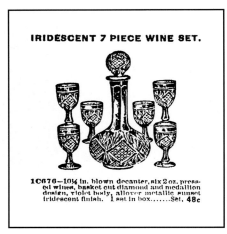

This ad for the **Diamond and Sunburst** wine set appeared in the spring 1911 issue of the Butler Brothers wholesale catalog.

**Shapes and Colors Known**

Wine decanter and stopper — marigold, purple
Stemmed wine — marigold, purple
Stemmed goblet — marigold

## Double Scroll

In many ways the Double Scroll pattern could also be considered a "double bridge." In color, it bridges the gap between carnival glass and stretch glass. Examples may be found with either type of iridescence. In style, the design appears to be an attempt to bridge the gap between Art Deco and Art Nouveau, a true reflection of the changing tastes of the 1915 – 1920 period.

Double Scroll was made in a three-piece console set comprised of a pair of 7" – 8" candlesticks and a matching console bowl. The bowl is dome footed, oval in shape, and quite large — about 12" in diameter from end to end. Marigold examples are easily found as are the clambroth sets. Smoke examples are very scarce, especially the console bowl. Most of the known examples in these three colors have a rich, carnival-type iridescence. Two other colors are known and both are very rare. Examples in a beautiful teal and a true, deep red sometimes shading to a yellow/amberina in the base, are known. Both of these colors usually exhibit the onion-skin effect of stretch iridescence.

Candlesticks have also been reported, though not confirmed, in helios. A punch cup has also been reported in marigold, but here again I cannot personally confirm its existence.

*Rare amberina **Double Scroll** three-piece console set.*

**Shapes and Colors Known**

Candlesticks — marigold, clambroth, smoke, teal, red, amberia, (helios?)
Console bowl — marigold, clambroth, smoke, teal, red, amberina
Punch cup (?) — marigold

## Etched Lustre

The Etched Lustre line of vases was actually part of a broader iridescent line that Imperial called their Lead Lustre assortments. The Balloons vase, pictured elsewhere in this book, was also part of this same line. Thirteen different vase shapes are illustrated in the old Imperial

*This marigold 6" **Etched Lustre** vase is one of 13 shape variations known in this line. There are also numerous styles of etchings found on these vases.*

factory catalogs. They include urn shapes, ovoid shapes, bud vases, and corset-shaped vases, all ranging in height from 6" to 12". All are very delicate, hand-blown vases that have been hand cut or etched in a variety of floral and stylized designs.

The catalog lists them as being available in Nuruby, Saphire, and Peacock. We know these colors today as marigold, smoke, and clambroth. Because of their delicacy, relatively few examples have survived the years, and they are not often found.

**Shapes and Colors Known**

Vases, 6" – 12", various shapes and etchings — marigold, smoke, clambroth

## Fancy Flowers

Known in only one carnival shape, Fancy Flowers is a very scarce Imperial pattern. It is seldom found and rarely mentioned in carnival glass collecting circles. It is listed in the factory catalogs as Imperial's #737.

The only shape known is a large, impressive, pedestal-footed bowl which many collectors call a compote. This busy, near-cut design is found on the exterior surface. The interior is plain. The short stem rises from the scalloped edged foot in distinct, graduated steps. The bowl measures from 8½" to 9½" in diameter and stands 4½" to 5" tall. Only a relative handful of marigold examples are known, and I can confirm at least one in helios. I would guess that this design would generate considerably more interest if a purple example were to surface.

This piece was reproduced in 1966 in marigold and smoke, trademarked with the IG logo.

*Some collectors call this shape a large compote, while others call it a pedestal-footed bowl. Regardless of what you call it, **Fancy Flowers** is a very scarce and underrated pattern.*

**Shapes and Colors Known**

Large bowl/compote, pedestal footed — marigold, helios

## Fashion

Originally listed in the factory catalogs as Imperial's #402½, Fashion is one of the most widely recognized near-cut type patterns in the entire field of carnival glass. Examples of this design make an outstanding addition to any collection. The shapes are impressive, the mold work and design is flawless, and the quality of the iridescence is superb. In fact, I don't recall ever seeing a poorly iridized example. A fairly extensive line of shapes and colors were produced, so the design must have been a popular one.

The marigold punch sets must have been especially popular. They are the most available of all the fashion shapes and are probably the most common of all carnival punch sets. Most of these punch bowls are ruffled, but a round, deep, non-ruffled version also exists. They are much harder to find than the ruffled examples. Virtually all other colors in the punch set are extremely rare. The punch bowl and base obviously exists in both purple and smoke, as cups are found in both of those colors. It also holds the distinction of being the only true carnival punch set known in red carnival. Several examples of the punch cup in red are known, and the matching punch bowl and base has now been reported.

*In configuration, this little **Fashion** breakfast creamer, in smoke, is an exact miniature of this impressive marigold water pitcher.*

Water sets in marigold are also quite plentiful. The smoke examples are very scarce, but do turn up from time to time. The purple sets are extremely rare, the iridescence on them often defies description, and they are highly treasured additions to any collection. Tumblers are also known in a beautiful, pastel clambroth, but to date, I have no confirmation of a matching pitcher. I can confirm the existence of at least one tumbler in an unusual, deep, rich, horehound-like, root beer color.

Particularly charming items in the Fashion line are the tiny, two-piece breakfast sets. They are comprised of a creamer, standing only 3½" tall, and a two-handled, open sugar. These sets are really seldom seen in any color, but the marigold is probably the most often found.

*Most **Fashion** pieces, like this rose bowl and two-piece breakfast set, are quite rare in purple.*

*Collectors call this type of bowl an ice cream shape. This absolutely stunning **Fashion** example in clambroth is actually a very rare shape for Imperial.*

Smoke examples are very scarce, but they can be found with a little patience. The helios and purple sets are extremely rare, with only a relatively few examples known.

Two shapes of bowls in the 9" size range are also known. Ruffled examples are quite common in marigold, but are rarely seen in smoke. The shallow ice cream-shaped bowls are much more difficult to find. They are known in marigold, clambroth, and a very scarce smoke. It seems strange that no other colors have been reported in the bowl shapes, especially when you consider the colors known in the next shape listed.

A large, collar-based rose bowl was shaped from the 9" bowl mold. It is, at the very least, quite scarce in any color, but is seen most often in marigold. Purple examples are extremely rare and desirable. The helios examples are rarer still, even though that color is not as popular with collectors. No other colors in the rose bowl shape have been reported.

The only other carnival shape known is a single example of a large, stemmed compote, reported only in smoke to date.

Like most of Imperial's geometric designs, Fashion was also produced in non-iridized crystal in a much wider range of shapes, including a four-piece table set. None of these have ever surfaced in carnival, but it is always possible that they might turn up.

As a general rule of thumb, most (but not all) Fashion pieces are fairly plentiful in marigold. Examples in virtually any other known color range from very scarce to extremely rare.

### Shapes and Colors Known

Punch set — marigold, purple, smoke, red
Water pitcher — marigold, purple, smoke
Tumbler — marigold, purple, smoke, clambroth, root beer
Breakfast set — marigold, purple, smoke, helios
Bowl, 9", ruffled — marigold, smoke
Bowl, 9", ice cream shape — marigold, smoke, clambroth
Rose bowl — marigold, purple, helios
Compote, large — smoke

## Fieldflower

Known only in a water set and a milk pitcher, Fieldflower was Imperial's #494 pattern. It is one of only three Imperial carnival patterns that are entirely floral in design.

The water sets are not too difficult to find in marigold. A little patient searching will usually turn one up. Helios examples are a little harder to find, but still show up in pretty fair numbers. The other colors will present more of a challenge. Amber examples are very scarce and, like most Imperial water sets, the purple ones are very rare. They are well worth the effort to find one, as they often exhibit spectacular iridescence. The top honors go to the cobalt blue pitchers. I do not recall one being sold at any of the carnival glass auctions, but a few extremely rare examples do exist. The matching tumblers are equally rare in blue.

Other colors are known, but only in the tumbler shape. Very scarce examples in olive have been reported. One of the most unusual is in a color called violet. At first glance, these examples appear to be blue. However, when held and turned in the light, distinct purple and lavender tones seem to magically appear. Only a relative few examples are known in this color. The number-one ranking goes hands down to the red tumbler. Yes, old red Fieldflower tumblers do exist. I can definitely confirm at least one example, and a second has been reported. They must be considered right up there on the top rare carnival tumbler list. No matching old water pitchers have yet surfaced in olive, violet, or red, but they likely do exist, so keep your eyes open for them.

The milk pitcher is very rare in any color. They have been reported in marigold, purple, and clambroth. I have heard of a helios example but have not been able to confirm it in that color. I do not recall of a Fieldflower milk pitcher changing hands at one of the carnival auctions for many years. Keep your eyes open for this rare treasure.

*Two views of **Fieldflower** water pitchers in very scarce amber and an absolutely magnificent purple.*

**Shapes and Colors Known**

Water pitcher — marigold, purple, helios, amber, blue
Tumbler — marigold, purple, helios, amber, blue, olive, violet, red
Milk pitcher — marigold, purple clambroth, (helios?)

## File

File was Imperial's #256 pattern. Prior to the carnival glass era, the design underwent extensive production in non-iridized crystal. An early factory catalog illustrates 22 different shapes. In carnival glass, the number of known shapes is far more limited.

Most collectors are familiar with File as an exterior design found on bowls with the Scroll Embossed interior pattern. In that form, File can be found in marigold, purple, helios, clambroth, and smoke.

When found as a primary pattern, the number of known shapes is far more extensive, but surprisingly, the range of colors known is very limited. A full, four-piece table set and a handsome water set are the best known of these shapes. They are quite rare and have been documented only in marigold to date.

Charming little whimsey vases, shaped from both the spooner mold and the base mold to the covered sugar, are also known. These are several shape variations. They may be ruffled, crimped, have a slightly corset shape, or even fashioned somewhat like a tiny spittoon. All are very rare and are known only in marigold.

The only other carnival shape reported is an impressive 11" chop plate. Here again. marigold is the only color reported, and this chop plate is very rare.

While these are the only iridized shapes reported, others are certainly possible. Non-iridized crystal shapes in the old factory catalogs include cruets, salt and pepper shakers, square bowls, banana bowls, tri-shaped bowls, cylindrical vases, and two sizes of flat plates. Any one of these shapes could well turn up in carnival.

No reproductions of this pattern are known to have been made.

*Marigold **File** tumbler and spooner.*

**Shapes and Colors Known**

*The rare **File** whimsey vase. This example was shaped from the mold for the base to the covered sugar bowl.*

Bowls, 5" – 9", Scroll Embossed interior — marigold, purple, smoke, clambroth, helios
Water set, table set, whimsey vase — marigold
Chop plate, 11 " — marigold
Bowl, 7" – 9" — marigold

## Floral and Optic

Floral and Optic is one of several Imperial designs that bridge the gap between carnival glass and stretch glass. It is found as a primary pattern and as an exterior design on Double Dutch footed bowls. Most examples in marigold, smoke, and clambroth have a rich, multi-color, carnival lustre. Most of the examples found in the other colors (of which there are many) carry a typical onion-skin, stretch effect to the iridescence.

Footed bowls in the 8" to 9" size range are the most available shape. Marigold and clambroth examples are rather scarce. Teal, white, and marigold on milk glass examples are very scarce, and will take a good deal of patient searching. Bowls in true red and red shading to amberina are also known. These are very rare and highly prized. The top honors go to the purple bowl. Only one example is known.

Large, 10" footed cake plates, shaped from the same mold, are also known. The colors here are more limited and all are really quite rare. Marigold and clambroth examples do turn up on occasion, but still, they are rarely found. Rarer still are the white and teal cake plates. Only a few are known. Red wins the rarity race, hands down. I have heard of only three or four examples.

The only other shape known is a footed rose bowl, here again shaped from the same mold. They are tough to find in any color, but marigold and clambroth seem to be the most often found. Examples in teal and smoke are probably the next most frequently seen color, but don't hold your breath while you're searching for one. They are very scarce. The marigold on milk glass examples are rarer still. The top ranking is a tough call. It's a case of actual rarity versus desirability. As far as the actual number of examples known is concerned, the celeste blue probably wins the race. Only a very few examples are known. There are probably a few more red rose bowls known, but they would no doubt win the popularity contest between the two colors. So take your pick. A Floral and Optic rose bowl in either color is an extremely rare find.

*Floral and Optic is one of the few Imperial patterns that can be found in marigold on milk glass, such as the scarce example shown here.*

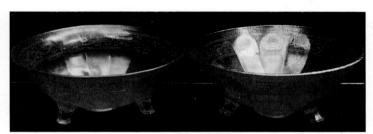

*The amberina Floral and Optic bowl on the left shades to yellow in the base. The example on the right is a deep, all-over cherry red.*

## Shapes and Colors Known

Bowl, footed, 8" – 9" — marigold, purple, clambroth, smoke, teal, white, marigold on milk glass, amberina, red
Cake plate, footed, 10" — marigold, clambroth, white, teal, red
Rose bowl, footed — marigold, clambroth, teal, smoke, marigold on milk glass, celeste blue, red

*Floral and Optic footed cake plate in white.*

*Several Floral and Optic shapes are featured in this assortment from the March 1924 Butler Brothers catalog.*

A great deal of confusion exists regarding Imperial's Flute. The true Imperial Flute pattern consists solely of items from the Imperial #700 line. Over the years, many items from the Chesterfield (#600) line, the Colonial (#593) line, and the Wide Panel line have been mistakenly called Imperial's Flute. It is time to clear this up once and for all.

Imperial's Flute is found in a variety of shapes that include punch sets, water sets, berry sets, toothpick holders, a celery vase, and a breakfast creamer and open sugar. The design was also used as an exterior pattern on Imperial's Heavy Grape pieces.

*This beautiful assortment of purple* **Imperial's Flute** *#700 includes the celery vase, toothpick holder, water pitcher, master berry bowl, and the two-piece breakfast set.*

**Flute** *variant #1 tumbler in purple.*

The punch set is identical in configuration to the Heavy Grape punch set, but lacks any interior pattern. The cups are sometimes signed with the Imperial Cross trademark. These sets are really quite rare in any color, but marigold examples are the most frequently found. Sets in helios and green are seldom seen and very underrated in value. The purple punch sets are a real treasure, with comparatively few complete sets known.

The berry sets have been reported only in marigold and purple. Even though the purple sets command the most attention, I must admit that I have seen more of them than I have of the marigold sets.

One of the most familiar items in the Flute #700 line is the charming little toothpick holder. It is very popular with collectors for good reason. It is found in a wider variety of colors than any other item in the Flute line. Marigold is the most often seen color, but a fair number of helios, emerald, and purple examples also turn up. The other known colors, which include aqua, vaseline, lime green, and cobalt blue, are all quite rare. These little beauties stand roughly 2¼" tall and are flared out at the top and base. There are six of the Flute panels.

The Flute celery vase is very rare and has been reported only in marigold and purple to date.

Nearly equal in rarity are the breakfast creamer and open sugar. They are most often seen in marigold or purple, but rare helios and emerald examples do exist.

Now we come to the Flute water set. This is an area that probably causes the most confusion of all, primarily because of several tumbler variations. We'll start with the water pitcher and then sort out the tumblers.

The Flute water pitcher is rarely encountered in any color. Marigold and purple are the most often found colors, but even they are very rare. Rarer still are the helios examples and the cobalt blue is ultra-rare, with only a couple of examples known.

It's really not too difficult to sort out the tumblers. The illustrations of the three variations shown here should help. Previous carnival references have listed as many as six Flute variants; however, three of these can be eliminated. The variants that were previously designated as Flute #s 4, 5, and 6 are *not* part of the Flute #700 line. They are actually part of the Chesterfield and Colonial lines. Some collectors may call me to task on this, but the original Imperial factory catalogs back me up.

*Flute* variant #2 tumbler in purple, really only a tankard version of the Flute #1 tumbler.

*Flute* variant #3 tumblers in purple, marigold, and helios.

FLUTE #1: This tumbler contains six Flute panels, the bottom is hexagonal in shape, and there is no collar base. The top and base are widely flared, giving the tumbler a somewhat corset shape. It is known in marigold, purple, and, surprisingly, at least one amber example is known. This tumbler measures from 3¾" to 4¼" tall, depending on how widely it is flared.

FLUTE #2: This tumbler also has six Flute panels, a hexagonal base, and has no collar base. It is much taller than the Flute #1, is straight sided, and has no flared top or bottom. It is, in effect, a larger, tankard version. It has been reported only in purple.

FLUTE #3: This tumbler is really the correct match to the Flute #700 water pitcher. Like the pitcher, there are nine of the Flute panels and it rests on a collar base. They have been found in all the matching colors — marigold, purple, helios, and cobalt blue. Very rare examples in aqua, smoke, and clambroth have also been confirmed. No matching pitchers have yet surfaced in these three colors, but they likely were made.

Many of the carnival glass producing firms often made and marketed tumblers individually — that is, sold separately without a matching water pitcher. Such is likely the case with regard to the Flute #1 and Flute #2 tumblers. Examples that do seem to mach them both appear individually in several different Butler Brothers Wholesale catalogs. It is also very possible that these two tumblers were at some point marketed with the Imperial Flute water pitcher as a rightful part of the set. We just don't know for sure.

All of the pieces described above are the only ones that are rightfully part of the true Imperial's Flute #700 line. Most of the other variants that have traditionally been called Imperial's Flute are actually pieces belonging to the Chesterfield (#600), Colonial (#593), and Wide Panel lines, which are shown elsewhere in this book.

Berry bowl, master — marigold, purple
Berry bowl, small — marigold, purple
Bowl, 7" – 8", mid size — marigold, emerald
Vase, 7", flared — marigold, cobalt blue
Breakfast creamer and sugar — Marigold, purple
Celery vase — marigold, purple
Punch bowl and base — marigold, purple, helios, green, emerald
Punch cup — marigold, purple, helios, green, emerald
Toothpick holder — marigold, purple, helios, green, emerald, aqua, vaseline, lime green, cobalt blue
Water pitcher — marigold, purple, helios, cobalt blue
Tumbler, Flute #1 — marigold, purple, amber
Tumbler, Flute #2 — purple
Tumbler, Flute #3 — marigold, purple, helios, cobalt blue, clambroth, aqua, smoke

# Flute and Cane
# (Cane)

Many carnival reference sources list Flute and Cane and Cane as two separate patterns. However, Imperial factory catalogs confirm that both are one and the same. The design carried the rather forboding designation of Imperial's #666. The catalogs also state that marigold was the only color available, and indeed, that is the only color documented for virtually all of the many shapes known.

Because there is only one color known for all shapes, there would be little sense in composing a lengthy text on this design. With only a couple of exceptions, all the shapes are very

*The **Flute and Cane** standard size water pitcher, which measures 8½" tall. The smaller milk pitcher is of identical configuration but is only 5¾" tall.*

*Two sizes of **Flute and Cane** tumblers. Both are extremely rare.*

scarce, at the least, and many of them are extremely rare. So I will list the known shapes along with their ranking as to rarity.

There are a few notes of interest that should be mentioned. The shape that we call a stemmed champagne was actually marketed as a fruit salad. The stemmed sherbet was often marketed with the 6" plate as a two-piece low ice cream set.

**Shapes and Colors Known**

All shapes reported only in marigold.

Bowl, 4½" – 7½"
Water pitcher, 8½" (scarce)
Milk pitcher, 5¾" (scarce)
Tumbler, 9oz. (extremely rare)
Tumbler, 12 oz. (extremely rare)
Plate, 6" (very scarce)
Sherbet, stemmed (scarce)
Cup and saucers (very rare)
Goblet, stemmed (scarce)
Wine, stemmed (rare)
Cordial, stemmed (extremely rare)
Breakfast creamer and sugar (very scarce)
Champagne, stemmed (rare)
Compote (scarce)

## Four Seventy Four

This design gets its name from the original factory pattern number, Imperial #474. The pattern is an unusual combination of molding techniques, combining relief-molded geometric

*The magnificent and extremely rare **Four Seventy Four** punch set. Very few of these purple sets are known.*

*Equally rare is this stunning **Four Seventy Four** water pitcher in purple.*

designs with an intaglio floral motif. It is the only Imperial carnival glass pattern that combines these two styles of molding.

The large, impressive water pitchers are a collector's favorite. They are still reasonably available in marigold. Virtually all of the other colors range from very scarce to extremely rare. Helios examples exist, but are very seldom found. The absolutely stunning purple water pitchers are one of the most eagerly sought of all Imperial carnival pitchers. Rarer still are the emerald pitchers. They often exhibit a brilliant, multicolor iridescence that rivals that of their purple counterparts. They have also been reported in a true olive color. This is probably the rarest color of all, but takes a back seat in desirability to the purple and emerald pitchers.

*This **Four Seventy Four** compote is also extremely rare in purple.*

*This special deal appeared in the August 1920 Butler Brothers catalog. It offers the **Four Seventy Four** punch set and water set, packed 12 sets to a barrel, for $18.00 wholesale, in marigold only. Many retailers likely took advantage of this offer, which would account for the availability of these marigold sets today.*

Tumblers exist in all of the above mentioned colors, plus a few others for which no matching water pitchers have yet been found. These colors include aqua, teal, lime green, cobalt blue, and violet. All are very rare, with cobalt blue and violet probably topping the list.

The smaller milk pitchers are found in marigold even more often than their big brothers. Here again, helios is scarce and the emerald and purple examples are very rare. Very rare olive examples also exist. They are also known in a beautiful, pastel lavender, which falls into the extremely rare category.

The Four Seventy Four punch set is also quite available in marigold. The other colors will present a challenge. The purple examples are very rare and highly treasured. At the top of the list in both rarity and beauty are the spectacular emerald punch sets. I know of only a handful of them and they are absolute knock-outs. I once owned one of them and sincerely regret ever parting with it. Rare examples also exist in a beautiful shade of aqua. I can also confirm punch cups and a couple of punch bowl bases in olive, so obviously the bowl must exist as well.

Five stemware shapes are also known in this design. These include scarce goblets, a rare wine glass, and an extremely rare, tiny, one-ounce cordial. The goblet is scarce in marigold and rare in helios or purple. The little cordial is known in marigold and purple. It is very rare in either color. The other stemmed shapes are a ruffled compote and a small sherbet. The ruffled compote is reasonably available in marigold, and extremely rare in purple. The sherbet has been reported only in marigold.

Pedestal-footed vases, in three sizes, are rarely found in any color. The 7" – 8" size vases have been reported in marigold and a single known example in true red. The 10" vase is reported only in marigold to date. The large 14" vase has been found in marigold and purple.

The only other carnival shape reported is an 8" – 9" collar-based, ruffled bowl. It is actually quite rare, and has been found only in marigold to date.

This pattern was reproduced during the 1960s and 1970s in a limited number of shapes and colors. The shapes made include the compote and vase. Also made was a large, handled mug, a shape not made in the old carnival line. The colors include marigold, smoke, pink, and red. All items were signed with the IG trademark.

### Shapes and Colors Known

Water pitcher — marigold, helios, purple, emerald, olive
Tumbler — marigold, helios, purple, emerald, olive, teal, aqua, lime green, cobalt blue, violet
Milk pitcher — marigold, helios, purple, emerald, olive, lavender
Punch bowl and base — marigold, helios, purple, emerald, aqua (olive base only)
Punch cup — marigold, helios, purple, emerald, aqua, olive
Goblet — marigold, purple, helios
Wine — marigold
Cordial — marigold, purple
Sherbet — marigold
Compote — marigold, purple
Vase, pedestal footed, 7" – 8" — marigold, red
Vase, pedestal footed 10" — marigold
Vase, pedestal footed, 14" — marigold, purple
Bowl, ruffled — marigold
Pitcher, mid size — marigold, purple

## Freefold

While some collectors call this pattern Interior Rays, I prefer the name Freefold, which was given to this design by Mr. Ray Notley of England. The name is a very appropriate and descriptive one. Besides, there are far too many Ray and Rib pattern names as it is. Adding yet another only adds to existing confusion.

This pattern is found only on the interior surface of beautiful, rather delicate-looking vases. The shaping of the top edges is often reminiscent of a daffodil. The exterior surface is smooth and unpatterned. These vases vary in height from 7" to as much as 14". There were apparently two different molds used to make them. One has a base diameter of 2⅞" with a 12-point star molded in the base, while the other has a base diameter of 3¼" with a 16-point star in the base. Examples of widely varying height may be found in either type base.

A beautiful, pastel lavender is the most frequently found color. Marigold and dark purple examples also turn up in fair numbers. The other colors are all rather scarce. They are, in order of rarity: pastel marigold, clambroth, helios, smoke, and surprisingly, white. Imperial made relatively little white carnival and examples of any of their patterns are rare in that color.

The quality of the iridescence on most examples ranges from excellent to outstanding, making the Freefold vase an attractive and affordable addition to any collection.

*Freefold vases in purple and marigold.*

**Shapes and Colors Known**

Vase, 7" – 14" — marigold, pastel marigold, lavender, helios, purple, clambroth, smoke, white

## Frosted Block

The iridized version of Imperial's #710, or Frosted Block as it is called today, came along rather late in the carnival production era. It does not appear in the wholesale catalogs until the 1920s. The variety of carnival shapes known is quite extensive; however, the range of colors known is very limited.

This is one of the Imperial carnival patterns that was exported in large quantities primarily to Central and South American countries. Many items can be found with the words, "MADE IN U.S.A." molded on the body of the piece, just above the lip of the collar base. These items were earmarked for export. They either found their way back to the States, or were never shipped, for reasons unknown.

The carnival production of this pattern was so extensive that even today, very few items could be classified as rare or even scarce. There are, of course, a few exceptions. The milk pitcher is a little tough to find in any color, and the pedestal-footed vase is very scarce in smoke. The square, 7" flat plate is also a toughie. Most of the other shapes are all quite available. The color most often seen in other shapes is a beautiful, pastel clambroth. Most shapes can also be found in a very pretty, frosty white. Surprisingly, true marigold examples are a little harder to find.

The design was reproduced in 1978 in pink carnival. These pieces were marked with the LIG logo.

**Shapes and Colors Known**

Bowl, round 5" – 7" — marigold, clambroth, white

Bowl, round 8" – 9" — Marigold, clambroth, white
Bowl, square 7" – 8" — Marigold, clambroth, white
Plate, round 9½" — marigold, clambroth, white
Plate, 7½", round — marigold, smoke, clambroth
Plate, square 7" — marigold, clambroth, white
Milk pitcher — marigold, clambroth
Creamer and open sugar, pedestal base — marigold, clambroth, white
Rose bowl, large, 3½" deep — marigold, clambroth, white
Rose bowl, small, 2½" deep — marigold, clambroth, white
Compote, stemmed — marigold, clambroth, white
Oval pickle dish, handled — marigold, clambroth, white
Vase, pedestal base 6" — clambroth, smoke

*Frosted Block* *milk pitcher in marigold, one of the harder items to find in this design.*

NOTE: This design was made in an even greater variety of non-iridized crystal shapes, so other carnival shapes are certainly possible.

*This* *Frosted Block* *rose bowl, in white, is also becoming a difficult item to find.*

## Gothic Arches

Only two examples of this very rare vase have been sold at the carnival glass auctions since 1983. One was 10" tall, and the other measured 11". Both examples were in smoke. As you can see, marigold examples also exist and are equally rare. Surely other colors must exist, but they have not been documented. Large, 17" funeral vases have also been reported.

This rare vase is included here as a likely Imperial product. We have no proof if its origin because almost nothing is known about it. However, Imperial produced about 90% of all smoke carnival glass, so this attribution seems probable. The known examples have a widely flared top, which is also typical of Imperial vases.

*The rare **Gothic Arches** vase in marigold.*

### Shapes and Colors Known

Vase, 10" – 17" — marigold, smoke
Vase, 14" – 18", funeral — marigold

## Hattie

Imperial's #496, or Hattie as it is called today, is an unusual blend of geometric, stylized, and naturalistic forms. Equally unusual is the fact that the design is duplicated on both the interior and exterior surfaces. Because of this unique feature, even the novice collector should have no trouble in recognizing this pattern.

Perfectly round, deep bowls are fairly abundant in marigold. The other colors are another story. Examples in helios and amber are the next most often encountered colors, but even these are quite scarce. Bowls in smoke are rare and the purple examples, even more so.

A rare rose bowl, shaped from the same mold, is also known. These have been reported only in marigold, purple, and amber. Large, flat 10" – 11" chop plates are the only other known shapes. They are really quite rare in any color, but marigold and clambroth seem to be the most often found colors A reasonable number of helios examples are also known. The chop plate in amber is very rare, but the top ranking goes to the purple examples. Comparatively few are known.

Reproductions of the bowl shape, all marked with the IG trademark, were made in smoke, green, pink, and white in the 1960s and 1970s.

## Shapes and Colors Known

Bowl, round, 8" — marigold, purple, helios, smoke, amber
Rose bowl — marigold, amber, purple
Chop plate, 10" – 11" — marigold, purple, helios, amber, clambroth

*This amber **Hattie** rose bowl is quite rare.*

*Relatively few examples of this handsome purple **Hattie** chop plate are known.*

*This marigold **Hattie** chop plate is a little easier to find, but still a pretty rare item.*

## Heavy Diamond

Were it not for existence of the pedestal-footed vase, this design would likely still be classed as "of unknown origin." Imperial produced more pedestal-footed vases of the style shown here than any other of the carnival glass producing firms. Add to that the fact that they

81

chose to produce nearly all of them in the same three colors — marigold, clambroth, and smoke, and it becomes quite evident that they are indeed Imperial products.

The Heavy Diamond vase is the most frequently encountered shape in this design. It has been reported in green and the three aforementioned colors. Still, they are quite scarce and often undervalued.

Other shapes reported in this pattern include 10" bowls, stemmed compotes, and a breakfast creamer and open sugar. The compote, like the vase, has been reported in green. All of the other shapes are known only in marigold.

***Heavy Diamond*** *vase in marigold.*

**Shapes and Colors Known**

Bowl, 10" — marigold
Compote — marigold, green
Creamer and sugar — marigold
Vase, pedestal footed — marigold, green, clambroth, smoke

## Heavy Grape

To avoid confusing this pattern with Dugan's Heavy Grape, the name Imperial's Heavy Grape should always be used. For many years this design was credited to Fenton. This probably stems from the fact that Fenton reproduced this design in the 1970s. They obviously must have purchased one of the molds from Imperial. The pattern does appear in early Imperial factory catalogs with the designation of Imperial's #700. This designation refers to the exterior Flute pattern. Imperial consistently designated their pattern numbers on the exterior design, regardless of the interior pattern.

Bowls are the most often encountered shape. They are found in three sizes, 5" – 6", 7" – 8", and large, 10" – 11". The two smaller sizes are quite available in marigold, purple, green, helios, and even emerald. The large bowls are very rare in smoke, aqua, amber, and light blue with a marigold overlay. They are also on rare occasion found in aqua and an extremely rare cobalt blue. The smaller bowls are known in smoke, and are extremely rare. In fact, the example pictured here is the only one known by this writer.

Flat plates, in the 7" – 8" size range, are also quite available in marigold, purple, green, helios, and emerald. They are rare in smoke and amber. A few extremely rare vaseline examples are also known.

Large, 11" – 12" chop plates are rarely encountered, but do turn up in marigold and, surprisingly, amber. Purple examples are far more difficult to find, as are the helios examples. They are also known in white, and are extremely rare with only a couple examples known. A single example in ice green has also been reported.

A small, 6" flat plate shaped from the mold of the 5" bowl is known in marigold.

A small, 4" – 5" single-handled nappy is relatively common in marigold. It is rarely found in purple and helios, and is actually extremely rare in olive.

A magnificent punch set is the only other shape known. They are very rare in marigold, and extremely rare in purple and helios. The punch cups have only a single leaf in the center, lacking any grapes. These punch cups are really one of the most difficult to find of all carnival punch cups. Topping the list is the amber punch set. Only a few are known.

The only reproduction of this pattern appears to be the 6" – 7" bowls that were made by Fenton in the 1970s. They are all marked with the Fenton logo, comprised of the word Fenton enclosed in an oval.

*The purple **Heavy Grape** master berry bowl is impressive.*

**Shapes and Colors Known**

Bowl, 5" – 6" — marigold, purple, emerald, helios, smoke, green
Bowl, 7" – 8" — marigold, purple, emerald, helios, smoke, green
Bowl, 9" – 10" — marigold, purple, emerald, helios, smoke, light blue, amber, aqua, cobalt blue, green
Plate, 6" — marigold
Plate, 7" – 8" — marigold, purple, emerald, helios, amber, smoke, vaseline, green
Chop plate, 11" – 12" — marigold, purple, emerald, helios, amber, smoke, white ice green, green
Nappy, handled — marigold, purple, helios, olive
Punch bowl and base — marigold, purple, emerald, helios, green, amber
Punch cup — marigold, purple, emerald, helios, green, amber

*Heavy Grape* 7" bowl in a beautiful, pastel smoke — a very rare color for this size.

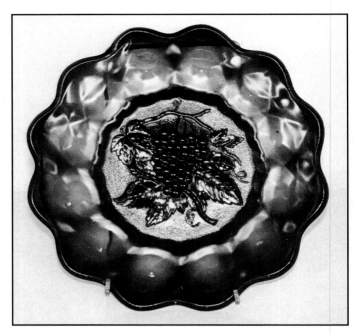

With a little patient searching, these purple *Heavy Grape* 8" plates can still be found.

This *Heavy Grape* 7" ruffled bowl is one of the more available pieces of Imperial's purple carnival.

Imperial's *Heavy Grape* pieces have the Flute #700 design as an exterior pattern. This example has a light blue base glass, with a marigold iridescent overlay.

## Heavy Grape Variant

To the best of my knowledge, this unusual variant of Imperial's Heavy Grape is shown and documented here for the first time. As you can see, there are several differences between this unusual plate and the standard version. This plate lacks the quilted diamond effect on the interior surface. The edge of the plate is not scalloped, but is completely smooth, with a distinctly 12-sided effect to it. This plate measures 8" in diameter. The Heavy Grape design in the center is identical to the one found on the standard Heavy Grape pieces. The color is a good, rich marigold.

The example shown is one of only two reported to date. I'm sure others, perhaps in other colors, must exist, but I have never seen one.

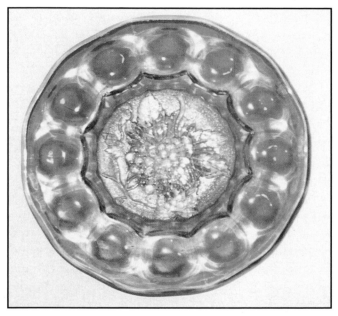

*Only two examples of this rare **Heavy Grape Variant** plate have been reported.*

**Shapes and Colors Known**

Plate, 8", twelve-sided — marigold

## Herringbone and Beaded Oval

What a curious situation exists regarding this design. The pattern is listed in the old Imperial factory catalogs as Imperial's #B-54½. Only one shape, a stemmed, ruffled compote, has been reported. They have been found only in marigold, and only a few examples are known.

It seems strange that Imperial seems to have produced only this compote, in old carnival. During the 1960s and 1970s, the design was reproduced in a wide variety of carnival shapes and colors. All were trademarked with the IG or LIG logos. The reproductions include handled baskets, covered candy dishes, compotes, bowls, and other shapes, in marigold, emerald, pink, red, and smoke.

The marigold compote, shown here, is the only known shape and color in old carnival.

*Only a few examples of the **Herringbone and Beaded Oval** compote are known.*

**Shapes and Colors Known**

Compote — marigold

## Hexagon and Cane

We are dealing with a pattern here that is so rare that a carnival glass example could not be located to photograph for this book. Most collectors are not even aware that the pattern exists. So the illustration of the pattern shown here, from an old Imperial factory catalog, will have to do, even though the shape illustrated has not been documented in carnival.

Hexagon and Cane was Imperial's #502 pattern and it was part of the NUCUT line. Several different shapes in non-iridized crystal exist. The only carnival shape known to date is a covered sugar, reported only in marigold. At present, only three examples are known and one of these is missing the cover. Other carnival examples likely exist, so be on the lookout for them.

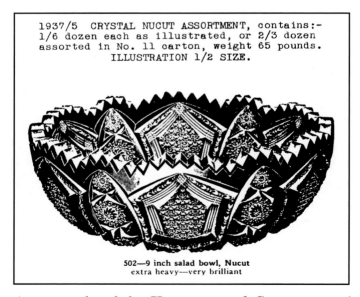

1937/5  CRYSTAL NUCUT ASSORTMENT, contains:-
1/6 dozen each as illustrated, or 2/3 dozen
assorted in No. 11 carton, weight 65 pounds.
ILLUSTRATION 1/2 SIZE.

502—9 inch salad bowl, Nucut
extra heavy—very brilliant

*An example of the **Hexagon and Cane** covered sugar could not be located for inclusion in this book, but the illustration shown here, from an old Imperial factory catalog, shows the pattern well.*

**Shapes and Colors Known**

Covered sugar — marigold

## Hobnail Soda Gold

Most collectors are probably familiar with the Hobnail Soda Gold spittoon in marigold. They are without question the most easily found of all carnival glass spittoons. What often comes as a surprise is that they are also found, on rare occasion, in amber, helios, and a true, frosty white. This large spittoon measures 7" in diameter and stands 4" tall. Many of them show considerable wear, indicating a good deal of actual use for the purpose of which they were intended. I have heard rumors of purple examples, but to date I cannot confirm them.

The only other confirmed shapes in this design are salt and pepper shakers, reported only in marigold. They are actually quite rare.

The **Hobnail Soda Gold** spittoon, in marigold, is the only carnival glass spittoon that is still easily found.

**Shapes and Colors Known**

Spittoon — marigold, helios, amber, white
Salt and pepper shakers — marigold

## Hobstar

Sometimes called Carnival Hobstar, this design appears in Imperial factory catalogs as Imperial's #282. Prior to the carnival era, this design underwent a more extensive production, in non-iridized crystal, than any other Imperial Glass pattern of the period. Over 60 different crystal shapes were produced.

The carnival glass version began to show up in the wholesale catalogs around 1912. While the variety of carnival shapes known is more limited, production of the shapes that are known must have been prolonged and extensive. With only a few exceptions, most carnival examples of the pattern are quite plentiful.

Bowls, in several sizes, are the most frequently seen items. The 9" and 5" – 6" sizes are the most frequently seen items. The 9" and 5" – 6" sizes make up an attractive berry set. Intermediate size bowls, in the 7" – 8" range, are also known. In all sizes, marigold examples are quite common. The purple bowls are harder to find, but do turn up.

The four-piece table set is also quite plentiful in marigold. In fact, it is probably the most available of all carnival glass table sets. The other colors are another story. The absolutely stunning purple sets are rare and seldom found. The emerald table set takes the top honors, though. Often encountered with a dazzling, multicolor iridescent lustre, they are extremely rare.

Large, covered cookie jars, standing roughly 8" tall, are also plentiful in marigold and very scarce in purple. A smaller version, standing about 1½" shorter, and listed in the factory catalogs as a covered milk jar, is also known in marigold. These are found somewhat less often than their larger cousins.

A rare, two-piece fruit bowl and base is also known in marigold and green. In recent years, very rare punch cups in marigold and green have surfaced, so this fruit bowl and base is, in all likelihood, actually the matching punch bowl and base.

Only three other shapes have been reported in carnival. A stemmed compote is known in marigold. A neat little pickle castor in a silver-plated metal frame is also known in marigold. A bride's bowl, comprised of a 9" ruffled bowl in a silver-plated metal frame is known in marigold. No other carnival shapes have been reported to date.

With so many non-iridized crystal shapes known, other carnival shapes are certainly possible. Some of the non-iridized shapes made include two styles of water pitchers, tumblers, wine decanters, stemmed wines, whiskey decanters, shot glasses, cruets, syrups, salt and pepper shakers, goblets, flat trays, handled nappies, and several sizes of bowls and flat plates. Any of these could well turn up in carnival.

The cookie jar and covered milk jar were reproduced in marigold and smoke in the 1960s. They are marked with the IG trademark.

*Hobstar* covered sugar, butter dish, and creamer in purple. These items are quite available in marigold, but purple is another story.

### Shapes and Colors Known

Bowls, 5" – 10" — marigold, purple
Table set — marigold, purple, emerald
Cookie jar — marigold, purple
Covered milk jar — marigold
Punch bowl and base — marigold, green
Punch cup — marigold, green
Compote, pickle castor, bride's bowl — marigold

## Hobstar and Arches

This geometric design shows many similarities to the Curved Star pattern. It almost appears to be a more refined version of Curved Star.

Imperial produced more different two-piece fruit bowl and base sets than any other carnival producing firm. Yet another exists in this design. It is a little harder to find than some of the others. A good, rich marigold is the usual color encountered, but helios examples turn up on occasion. They have also been reported in purple, and as is the case with most Imperial fruit bowls, these are quite rare in that color. These bowls generally measure 11" to 12" in diameter, and most examples are deeply ruffled.

An interesting situation exists here with regard to the base to the fruit bowl. It was used with two different fruit bowls and one punch bowl. Even though this base carries the Hobstar and Arches pattern, it is also the correct base to accompany the Long Hobstar fruit bowl and the Royalty punch bowl. Imperial certainly got a lot of mileage out of this mold.

Slightly smaller, 8½" to 9½" ruffled bowls are also known in marigold, helios, purple, and smoke. Only the marigold examples are found in any quantity. The others are all quite rare.

*Hobstar and Arches 8½" bowl in marigold.*

### Shapes and Colors Known

Bowl, 8½" – 9½" — marigold, purple, helios, smoke
Fruit bowl and base — marigold, purple, helios

## Hobstar and Tassels

Most collectors are not familiar with this unusual, geometric design, as relatively few examples are known. It consists of four large hobstars surrounded by swirling, zipper-like tassels, and is found only on the exterior surface of 7" – 9" bowls. The interior surface may be plain or carry the Scroll Embossed pattern.

Round, deep, 7" bowls with a sawtooth edge are the most frequently encountered shape. These have been found in purple and helios. The iridescence on the purple examples is often stunning. Ruffled 9" bowls in two shape variations are also known. Some have six ruffles and some have eight. These ruffled bowls are very typical of Imperial and have a smooth edge. These have been found in purple, helios, and a rare and beautiful shade of teal. No marigold examples, in any of these shapes, have yet been confirmed, but they likely do exist.

There has been some speculation that this pattern is of English origin. I had always doubted this, primarily because no marigold examples have surfaced. Most English carnival is found primarily in marigold. In addition, the known helios examples are typical of Imperial, and no English carnival has ever surfaced with this type of iridescent treatment. We can now conclusively confirm that Hobstar and Tassles is an Imperial creation. The pattern is featured prominently in an Imperial factory catalog, dated 1909.

***Hobstar and Tassels***, *found only on the exterior of some Scroll Embossed bowls, and bowls with a plain interior.*

**Shapes and Colors Known**

Bowl, 7 round, sawtooth edge — purple, helios
Bowl, 9" ruffled, smooth edge — purple, helios, teal

## Hobstar Flower

For many years this design has been credited to Northwood. Most carnival references still list it as a Northwood product. Exactly why remains a mystery to me. In shape, size, design characteristics, molding, and quality of iridescence, it bears virtually no resemblance to any other Northwood creations. The colors in which it is found, along with the brilliant, radium type of iridescence found on most examples simply *screams* Imperial at you!

Stemmed, ruffled compotes, standing roughly 5" to 5½" tall, are the only shapes known. A deep, rich purple, often exhibiting dazzling iridescence, is the most often found color, but even these are very rarely seen. Marigold examples are much harder to find. Helios examples, further evidence of an Imperial origin, are also known. These are really quite rare. I have seen only four or five of them over the years. Rarer still are the beautiful emerald compotes. I have seen only two, and both had spectacular, multicolor iridescence. Cobalt blue examples have been rumored to exist, but to date I cannot confirm them.

A smoke example would certainly nail down the Imperial attribution, but none have ever surfaced.

***Hobstar Flower*** *compotes in purple and helios. This helios example almost bridges the gap in iridescent lustre between helios and emerald.*

**Shapes and Colors Known**

Compote — marigold, purple, helios, emerald

## Hoffman House

Just about every major glass factory produced a non-iridized version of the famous Hoffman House style of goblet. They appear in factory catalogs from McKee, Federal, U.S. Glass, Imperial, and a whole host of others. This simple, utilitarian goblet was (and still is) a very popular fixture in restaurants, hotels, and taverns.

Back in the late teens or early twenties, Imperial produced a very limited run of these goblets in carnival. Few collectors have ever seen one or are even aware that they exist. I would doubt that more than a dozen are known. The only color reported is a deep, rich amber with a brilliant multicolor iridescence.

*The rare carnival version of the*
***Hoffman House*** *goblet.*

**Shapes and Colors Known**

Goblet — amber

## Homestead

Make no mistake about it, this is one of the rarest and most desirable of all Imperial carnival glass patterns. This was Imperial's #525 pattern and the design was quite obviously created by the same artist responsible for the Windmill and Double Dutch patterns. It is found only on the interior of large, 10½" chop plates. The exterior surface is ribbed. Some examples are found with the NUART trademark, but some are found unsigned as well.

These beautiful examples of the moldmarker's art are very seldom found in any color, but marigold examples do turn up now and then. The amber and purple plates are seen less often, but still surface on occasion. Helios examples are quite rare and the white and smoke plates even more so. The top honors here go to the cobalt blue examples. Only a few are known. A close second in rarity would be the stunning emerald examples. They have also been reported in olive. These are also very rare, but this color seems to be one of the least popular, so their value is considerably less. The way things are on the carnival glass market today, the bottom line is simply this: the Homestead plate is a rare find in any color. Very few examples surface outside of the carnival glass auctions.

This plate was widely reproduced in the 1960s and 1970s. The new plates have a plain exterior and were trademarked with the IG logo. Reproduction colors include marigold, smoke, amber, helios, and white. A newer reproduction in vaseline by the Summit Art Glass Company is now on the market.

*Purple **Homestead** chop plate.*

**Shapes and Colors Known**

Chop plate, 10½" — marigold, purple, helios, amber, smoke, white, cobalt blue, emerald, olive

# Imperial's Basket

We call this simply Imperial's Basket, so that it is not confused with the numerous other similarly shaped baskets that Imperial produced. Besides, the name is most appropriate for a design consisting of a woven basket. This 10" tall handled basket is much harder to find than most of its other, similar cousins. Only three colors have been reported, and all range from very scarce to extremely rare. Marigold examples are the most available. Smoke examples are rarely encountered. Topping the rarity list are the marigold on milk glass baskets. Only a few are known, and they rarely change hands.

**Shapes and Colors Known**

Handled basket, 10" — marigold, smoke, marigold on milk

*The **Imperial Basket** is a very scarce item, even in marigold.*

## Imperial Paperweight

This very rare piece of carnival glass was obviously made as a souvenier, perhaps to be given to visitors to the Imperial factory. This solid, rectangular paperweight is 5½" long, 3⅛" wide, and roughly 1" thick. Molded along one side are the words, "Imperial Glass Company, Bellaire, Ohio, USA." The opposite side is molded with the words, "Imperial Art Glass." The center of the paperweight is depressed and molded with three of Imperial's trademarks, the Nuart and Nucut logos, and the famous Imperial Cross mark. Very few of these paperweights exist and all known examples are in purple.

*Two views of the extremely rare **Imperial Paperweight**.*

The three trademarks molded in the center may offer some clues as to when this item was made. The Nuart trademark dates from about 1911. The patent for the Nucut trademark was granted on September 15, 1914. The patent for the Imperial Cross mark was filed on the same date; however, the letters spelling out the word Imperial were not added until much later. A patent for the complete, lettered version of the Imperial Cross mark was not granted until August 16, 1921. It therefore seems likely that the Imperial paperweight may have been made at about that time.

**Shapes and Colors Known**

Paperweight — purple

## Imperial's Grape

Just over the river from Bellaire, Ohio, was the town of Wheeling, West Virginia. There in 1910 Harry Northwood introduced his most famous carnival creation, the Grape and Cable line. The design proved to be a tremendously popular one, so obviously Imperial would have to counter with a similar line of their own. The result was Imperial's #473 pattern or Imperial's Grape, as we now call it. It was the most extensively produced pattern, in both shape and color variety, of all Imperial carnival designs. At least 25 different shapes are known in a wide variety of colors.

This certainly gives today's collector plenty to hunt for. The design must have been nearly as popular as Northwood's Grape and Cable. While there are items that fall into the extremely rare category, many of the shapes and colors can still be found, and at reasonable price levels. A very impressive collection, devoted solely to Imperial's Grape, can still be assembled. Not only are many of the items in this line still available, the iridescence on most of them is superb. You will find very few poorly iridized pieces.

With so much to cover and discuss, we will take a slightly different format approach here. We will take all of the known shapes, one at a time, and present the information regarding color and rarity.

Large ruffled bowl, collar base, 10" – 12" — These are a little on the scarce side in any color, but surprisingly, the stunning purple examples are the most often seen. Marigold examples are harder to find. The are also reported in a beautiful shade of lavender. The positively magnificent emerald examples are extremely rare. Very rare in cobalt blue.

*Is it any wonder why Imperial's purple carnival glass is so eagerly sought? Just look at the rich, beautiful iridescence on this **Imperial's Grape** punch set and equally magnificent water set. Both are rare, but not as much so as other Imperial sets in purple.*

Small ruffled bowl, collar base, 4" – 5" — These are not really found all that often, but turn up the most in marigold. The purple, lavender, and emerald examples are quite scarce. They are also known in amber and a very rare violet.

Master berry, round, deep, 8" – 9½" — Quite easily found in marigold, helios, and even amber. They are scarce in lavender or clambroth. Ultra-rare is the marigold on milk glass, with only a couple of examples known. Purple examples are seldom found.

Small berry, round, deep, 4" – 5" — Easily found in marigold, helios, and amber. Purple and clambroth are scarce. Only a couple violet examples reported.

Bowl, ruffled, collar base, 8" – 9" — Easily found in marigold and helios. Purple examples are a little tougher, but still turn up in fair numbers. Scarce in clambroth, amber, and lavender. Very rare in emerald and smoke. One, ultra-rare cobalt blue bowl is known. A red example has also been rumored to exist, but I cannot confirm this as of this writing.

*Only two examples of this cobalt blue **Imperial's Grape** 6" flat plate have been reported, making it one of the rarest of all Imperial carnival glass plates.*

*This handsome, **Imperial's Grape** 12" collar-based fruit bowl, in purple, can still be found with a little patient searching.*

*The **Imperial's Grape** compote is rare in olive.*

*The **Imperial's Grape** water set, berry set, compote, and punch cup are featured in this assortment from the April 1915 Butler Brothers catalog.*

*Imperial's Grape decanter and wine glass in marigold. The Butler Brothers ad for this set appeared in the April 1912 catalog.*

Bowl, low ruffled, 8" – 9" — Some call this a ruffled plate. I am of the old school of thought: If it is ruffled, it is not a true plate, regardless of how low it is. These are seen far less often than the previously listed shape. They are rather scarce in any color, but are known in marigold, purple, helios, clambroth, and lavender.

Nut bowl, collar base — This bowl is roughly 4½" – 5" deep, with a diameter of about 6". It is very rare and has been reported only in marigold.

Rose bowl, collar base — Shaped from the 8" – 9" bowl mold. Very rare in any color. To date, it has been reported only in marigold, helios, and amber. Purple likely exists, but is unconfirmed.

Plate, 6" — One of the widest varieties of colors exists here. It is easily found in marigold, but scarce in helios, amber, and purple. It is very scarce in lime green and very rare in emerald, olive, and especially teal. Only a couple of extremely rare examples in cobalt blue are known.

Plate, 9" — Though harder to find than the small plate, marigold examples are reasonably plentiful. Helios is the next most often seen and the amber plates are scarce. The purple plates are very rare and are highly treasured. A few very rare examples in aqua and a beautiful emerald are also known. The top honor goes to the smoke plates. I know of only two examples. Some of these plates have been found with the Imperial Cross mark.

Cup and saucer — One of the few true cup and saucers known in old carnival. The saucer is very flat with the edge turned up. The interior of the saucer has a Smooth Rays pattern. The cup is the same as the punch cup. It is scarce in marigold and very rare in helios, amber, and purple.

Stemmed compote — Easily found in marigold and a fair number of helios examples turn up. Scarce in amber, very rare in purple, and extremely rare in smoke and olive.

Basket, handled 10" — Same basic shape as most other Imperial baskets described in this book. Rather scarce in any color, but turns up most often in marigold. Clambroth is harder to find and smoke examples are quite rare. To date, no other colors have been reported. A purple example would be a real find.

Punch bowl and base — Still easily found in marigold and not too difficult to find in helios. Purple examples are quite spectacular and highly prized. They are very seldom found. Examples in amber are also known and these are very rare. A single example in cobalt blue can now be confirmed. No matching base or cups have yet surfaced, but they must surely exist. A punch bowl and base has also been reported in smoke, but remains unconfirmed.

Punch cup — Same colors and rarity as the punch bowl.

Water pitcher — Very easily found in marigold, and helios examples turn up in fair numbers. Purple examples bring respectable prices and are highly prized, but are actually one of the more available Imperial water pitchers in that color. Examples in amber and smoke are very rare and always bring top dollar. Examples in a beautiful, pastel aqua are also known, and are extremely rare. The top ranking goes to the emerald pitchers. They are positively breathtaking, with a dazzling, multicolor, radium iridescence. Only three or four are known, and I deeply regret ever parting with the one I once owned.

Tumbler — An even wider variety of colors known here. There are two variants, one with a plain interior and one with a ribbed interior. The ribbed interior is harder to find. This tumbler is quite easy to find in marigold and helios, and not really too tough in purple. The others all range from very scarce to extremely rare. Amber is very scarce, while examples in lavender, smoke, lime green, and aqua are very rare. Examples in vaseline and emerald are extremely rare. The top spot goes to the ice green tumbler. I know of only one example! No matching pitchers in vaseline, lime green, or ice green have been reported.

Wine decanter and stopper — Buy these with the stopper intact whenever you can. The delicate, hollow stoppers are just about impossible to find. This decanter is still quite available in marigold, and even the helios examples still turn up. The purple ones are getting scarce, especially with the stopper intact. Examples in clambroth are harder to find and the emerald ones are rare. Rarest of all is the smoke. Relatively few are known.

Stemmed wine — Easily found in marigold and helios. Examples in purple, emerald, and clambroth are getting hard to find. They are very rare in olive and smoke. They are extremely rare in cobalt blue, with only a couple examples known. No matching decanter has yet surfaced in olive or cobalt blue.

Stemmed goblet — Rather scarce in any color, but marigold examples do turn up. Hard to find in helios, clambroth, and amber. Rare in purple and very rare in smoke and aqua.

Water carafe — Imperial factory catalogs actually list this as a vase, but it is shaped exactly like a carafe or water bottle. The shape is identical to the wine decanter, but it has a widely flared top and, of course, there is no stopper. These are very scarce in any color, but surprisingly, the beautiful purple examples are the most often found. Examples in clambroth and helios are much harder to find. Emerald and smoke examples are quite rare, and the beautiful aqua carafes are very rare. The big surprise here is that the marigold carafe is one of the hardest of all to find.

Whimsey spittoon — These were shaped from the 8" – 9" bowl mold. Only two colors, marigold and helios, have been reported and either one is extremely rare.

Handled nappy — Very rare. Reported in marigold, purple, and helios to date.

Electric light shade — Bell shaped. Quite rare and reported only in marigold.

With such an extensive production, other carnival shapes and colors are a definite possibility. New finds are constantly being reported in this pattern. In fact, the nut bowl only surfaced a couple of years ago. The Imperial's Grape Variant bowl, shown elsewhere in this book, turned up while this book was being written. So be on the lookout for other shapes and colors. The possibilities are almost limitless.

Imperial reproduced this design quite extensively in the 1960s and 1970s. A wide variety of shapes, including many not originally produced in old carnival, were made. You will find several of these new shapes illustrated in the section of this book on reproductions. Colors made include marigold, smoke, purple, helios, aurora jewels, and amber.

Several of the Imperial's Grape molds are now owned by other glass companies, including Wetzel Glass and the Summit Art Glass Company. New carnival examples are now on the market. Colors include electric blue, vaseline, red, and an unusual iridized opaque custard color. There are likely others.

## Imperial's Grape Variant

Imperial's Grape Variant is documented and shown here for the very first time. The marigold bowl shown here is the only known example of the pattern. It is 7½" wide, stands 2½" deep, and has a collar base diameter of 3". The interior of the bowl is plain, with no pattern whatsoever. A single, large grape leaf is molded on the underside of the collar base. The exterior design is the same as that found on the standard version of Imperial's Grape.

There are several possibilities concerning the origin of this unusual piece. It may be the result of a retooled mold, but I tend to doubt this. The underside of the collar base on the standard Imperial's Grape bowls is plain. Why retool a grape leaf onto an unpatterned area that would show no signs of wear in the first place?

A second possibility is that the piece could be of European origin. Imperial shipped considerable quantities of carnival glass to Europe from about 1911 onwards. Market and Company of England was their importing agent. Subsequently, during the 1920s and early 1930s, at least two European firms are known to have produced carnival glass copies of several Imperial patterns. So it *is* possible that this piece could have been made in Europe and found its way back here.

The third possibility is the one that I feel is the most probable. This bowl could be a surviving test piece for the mold. After it was made, it was decided that the design needed more to it. The grape leaf was removed from the base mold and the familiar interior design found on all other examples of Imperial's Grape was added. I feel that this may be the most likely scenario. If the bowl were of European origin, surely more examples would be known.

**Shapes and Colors Known**

Bowl, 7½" — marigold

*Imperial's Grape Variant*

## Little Barrel

There is little doubt that these unique little novelty bottles were made for special order customers rather than for the general trade. They do not appear in any of the known issues of the wholesale catalogs. Examples have been found with paper labels intact with the name of a business on them. In at least one case, the name on the label proved to be that of a tavern. So it is virtually certain that they contained some form of alcoholic beverage and were given as premiums.

Marigold examples seem to be the most often found, followed closely by smoke. Helios examples are harder to find, but will usually not command the attention or value of the more readily available smoke. Some examples almost cross the line between helios and emerald, exhibiting a more vibrant, multicolor iridescence. These will, of course, command a much better price. The Little Barrel has also been reported in amber, but at present I cannot confirm this. In 26 years of carnival collecting, I have never seen one.

These little bottles are not that easily found in any color.

***Little Barrels*** *in smoke, marigold, and helios.*

**Shapes and Colors Known**

Barrel-shaped bottle — marigold, smoke, helios (amber?)

## Loganberry

The Loganberry vase is listed in the Imperial factory catalogs as Imperial's #477. The bottle-necked, carafe shape standing 10" tall combines beautifully with the outstanding quality of the mold work. Add to that the magnificently rich iridescent lustre that is found on most examples, and you have a real collector's favorite. They are not easily found in any color.

Surprisingly, the colors that seem to be the most often encountered are helios and amber. Emerald examples, rare in most Imperial carnival patterns, also surface in fair numbers. This is a most unusual situation. Marigold examples are actually harder to find than the aforementioned three colors. The absolutely stunning purple vases are a sight to behold. The are very rare and highly treasured. I do not recall a smoke example ever changing hands at any of the carnival glass auctions, but they most definitely do exist. They are listed as one of the available colors in the old Imperial factory catalogs, so they were surely made. They would have to take the top ranking in rarity.

There are also a couple of whimsey-shaped vases known. A single amber example is known with the top of the vase flared straight out. A purple example, with a most unusual shaping to the top portion, is also known. The top is shaped into a ball-like form, not unlike the shape of a rose bowl. No other carnival shapes have been reported.

The Loganberry vase was reproduced in the 1960s and 1970s. The colors made include marigold, smoke, helios, and white. All were marked with the IG trademark.

*Loganberry vase in purple.*

**Shapes and Colors Known**

Vase, 10" — marigold, purple, helios, emerald, amber, smoke
Whimsey vase, flared top — amber
Whimsey vase, ball-shaped top — purple

## Long Hobstar

This is yet another of Imperial's geometric designs that was produced in huge quantities over an extended period of time. Marigold examples are abundant, so the design must have been a popular seller.

The marigold two-piece fruit bowl and base is one of the most easily found in the entire carnival glass field. Examples are also known in helios, and these are really quite rare. The bowl has also been reported in smoke, but to date, no matching base has been confirmed. At the top of the rarity list is the purple fruit bowl. Only one example is known. Most examples are deeply ruffled, but round, deep fruit bowls do exist. While some have called these punch bowls, no matching cups have ever surfaced. The top diameter of the fruit bowl usually measures in the 11" to 12" range. The base to this fruit bowl is the same one used for the Hobstar and Arches fruit bowl and base.

Smaller, 8" – 9" ruffled bowls are also known, primarily in marigold. However, rare examples in helios and purple are also found on occasion. Some of these bowls are occasionally found in a silver-plated metal holder. They make a most attractive bride's bowl. No other carnival shapes are known.

*Exterior view of the only known **Long Hobstar** fruit bowl in purple.*

### Shapes and Colors Known

Bowl, 8" – 9" — marigold, helios, purple
Bride's bowl in holder — marigold, helios, purple
Fruit bowl and base — marigold, helios, purple, smoke (bowl only reported in smoke and
    purple)

## Lustre Rose and Open Rose

For many years, these two patterns have been listed separately in most carnival reference sources. The so-called Open Rose plates and bowls have always been considered as a separate design. I never thought that they were, and the old Imperial factory catalogs have confirmed my belief. Both designs are illustrated together under the designation of Imperial's #489 pattern. Open Rose is nothing more than the collar-based bowl and plate version of the Lustre Rose pattern.

Lustre Rose was one of the most extensively produced Imperial carnival glass patterns. To date, we can document at least 18 shapes, many of them found in a wide range of colors. Many collectors have taken this pattern for granted. They are unaware of the tremendous color variety that exists in many of the shapes, thinking only of marigold or helios when the name Lustre Rose is mentioned. Perhaps the following will change that and spark some new interest in the design.

We'll start with the footed fernery, which is known in one of the widest variety of colors. Everyone is familiar with the marigold examples, as they are abundant. Even the purple and helios examples are not all that difficult to find. Surprisingly, neither are the cobalt blue examples. They are one of the more plentiful Imperial carnival pieces to be found in that color. Now, for a few surprises. Few collectors probably realize that this fernery is also known in amber, aqua, teal, clambroth, olive, smoke, amberina, and a beautiful, frosty white. All of these are rare, but the amber and clambroth examples can be found with a little searching. The smoke, teal, aqua, and olive examples are quite rare. The top spot is shared by the extremely rare white and amberina examples. The beautiful amberina fernery shades from a deep red color to a brilliant yellow/vaseline tint. Only a couple of examples are known.

Two other shapes were fashioned from the same mold. An ice cream bowl-shaped centerpiece bowl exists, and it is quite rare in any color. They are known in marigold, helios, clambroth, amber, and smoke, with the smoke examples the hardest to find. A footed, flat whimsey plate was also fashioned from this same mold. It is very rare and has been reported only in marigold to date.

Other bowl shapes include a collar-based berry set, usually round and deep in shape. They are quite easily found in marigold, helios, and even amber. The magnificent purple examples are rare and seldom found. They are ultra-rare in cobalt blue, but they do exist. Rare examples are also known in aqua, smoke, vaseline, and an unusual shade of light smokey blue with a marigold iridescent overlay.

*The spectacular iridescence on this purple **Lustre Rose** water set makes this a stunning addition to any collection.*

*A very rare vaseline **Open Rose** 8" bowl.*

Collar-based, 7½" – 9" bowls, either round or ruffled, are often referred to as Open Rose. Several variations in pattern detail are found on these bowls, indicating the use of several different molds. The outer edge of the interior pattern may be either plain or ribbed. The positioning of the roses, buds, and leaves may vary considerably. The exterior surface of the center portion of the collar base may be plain or patterned with a large rose. Some controversy surrounds the variant with the large rose molded on the underside of the collar base. In recent years a rumor has circulated that these pieces are unsigned reproductions. There is absolutely *no truth* to these rumors. I have seen and owned, over the years, many examples both with and without the molded rose in the base. In many cases, I know where the pieces came from and there is no question about their age. This variant is simply the result of a different exterior mold plate being used. Bowls in Open Rose are most often found in marigold and helios. Amber examples are harder to find and the magnificently iridized purple bowls are scarce. Topping the rarity list is a single known example in a beautiful, pastel lavender.

The 8" – 9" footed, ruffled-edge bowl is one of the more familiar shapes in this pattern. They are easily found in marigold and helios, and not too difficult to find in clambroth or even amber. Purple examples are harder to find, and smoke even more so. They have also been reported in a rare olive. The top ranking, in my opinion, goes to the vaseline examples. I only know of two, and believe me, I'm sorry that I ever sold mine.

A complete four-piece table set was made and it is very easily found in marigold. Helios sets are harder to find. The purple table set is very rare and seldom seen. Rarer still are the beautiful amber table sets. The creamer and spooner have also been reported in aqua, so full sets likely exist in this color as well. They have also been found in light blue with a marigold iridescent overlay.

There are two versions of the water set. The standard version has a ribbed interior on both the pitcher and tumblers, and a rayed star molded in the base. They are easily found in marigold and even helios. They are very rare and desirable in purple and are often found with a dazzling electric iridescence. Rarer still are the deep, rich amber water sets. Relatively few are known.

The standard tumbler with the ribbed interior is also known in aqua and olive. To date, I have not been able to confirm pitchers in those two colors. Rare smoke tumblers also exist.

The Lustre Rose Variant water set has a plain interior and a plain base, lacking both the ribbing and the rayed star. Strangely, the water pitcher has been documented in only two colors — marigold and clambroth — to date. The Variant tumblers have been documented in marigold, clambroth, aqua, light blue with a marigold iridescent overlay, lime green, and an ultra-rare, true, frosty white. Surely the matching water pitchers for these colors must be out there, somewhere. No variant pitchers or tumblers have been confirmed in purple, helios, or amber either. The Lustre Rose Variant pitchers and tumblers are much harder to find than the standard version.

*This **Open Rose** 9" plate, in amber, is a scarce and often underrated item.*

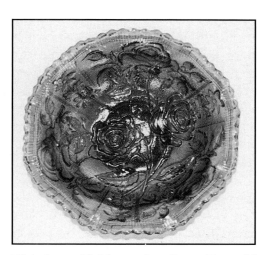

*This beautiful lavender **Open Rose** 8" bowl is the only one known.*

*While most Imperial carnival is extremely rare in cobalt blue, the **Lustre Rose** fernery seems to turn up frequently.*

*This unusual smoke **Open Rose** rose bowl certainly proves that green was not the only color that the helios iridescent treatment was applied to.*

The 9" flat plate is often referred to as Open Rose. These were fashioned from the same molds used for the 7½" – 9" collar-based bowls, hence the same variations in pattern detail apply here as well. They are one of the more available carnival plates in marigold and helios. Clambroth examples also turn up from time to time. Amber examples are really quite scarce and much underrated. The magnificent purple plates are rarely found and are a real treasure. They often exhibit a fantastic, multicolor iridescence. With such a wide variety of colors known in the other shapes in this design, surely plates in other colors will one day surface.

A collar-based rose bowl was fashioned from the same mold used for the collar-based bowls and plates. These are easily found in marigold, helios, and even amber. The fabulous purple rose bowls are another story. They are very rare, and always much in demand. During the writing of this book, an example of the rose bowl surfaced in smoke, and I am pleased to be able to show it here, for the first time. To the best of my knowledge, it is the only one known.

The large, footed 11" – 12" fruit bowls are quite common in marigold and clambroth. They are scarce in helios and even more so in smoke. The purple fruit bowl is a very rare and desirable item. Very rare examples in aqua and vaseline have also been reported. The top honors go to the true, red Lustre Rose fruit bowls. Only two are known, and only one of these is in perfect condition. Light blue with a marigold iridescent overlay is the only other reported color here.

The only other carnival shape known is an extremely rare whimsey vase fashioned from the tumbler mold. This vase stands 3½" tall with the top flared to 5" diameter. Two examples, one in clambroth and the other in light blue with a marigold iridescent overlay, have been reported.

Perhaps by now you are beginning to gain a new respect and appreciation for this much taken for granted pattern. With such a tremendous variety of colors and shapes, the collecting potential is astounding. There is certainly an awful lot here to hunt for and enjoy.

This pattern was reproduced in the 1960s and 1970s. A wide variety of shapes, including an 11" chop plate, an item not originally made in old carnival, were produced. The colors made include marigold, smoke, helios, purple, amber, meadow green, white, red, and pink. All items were trademarked with either the IG, LIG, or ALIG logos.

### Shapes and Colors Known

Fernery, footed — marigold, purple, helios, amber, olive, clambroth, aqua, cobalt blue, amberina, smoke, white
Centerpiece bowl, footed — marigold, helios, amber, smoke, clambroth
Whimsey plate, footed — marigold
Berry bowl, large — marigold, purple, helios, amber, aqua, cobalt blue, smoke, vaseline, light blue with marigold overlay
Berry bowl, small — marigold, purple, helios, amber smoke, cobalt blue, aqua
Bowl, collar base, 7½" – 9" — marigold, purple, helios, amber lavender
Bowl, footed, 8" – 9" — marigold, purple, helios, amber, smoke, olive, vaseline
Butter dish — marigold, purple, helios, amber, light blue with marigold overlay
Covered sugar — marigold, purple, helios, amber, light blue with marigold overlay
Water pitcher, standard — marigold, purple, helios, amber
Tumbler, standard — marigold, purple, helios, aqua, amber, olive, smoke
Water pitcher, variant — marigold, clambroth
Tumbler, variant — marigold, clambroth, teal, lime green, aqua, light blue with marigold overlay, white
Plate, 9" — marigold, purple, helios, amber, clambroth
Rose bowl — marigold, helios, purple, amber, smoke
Large footed fruit bowl, 11" – 12" — Marigold, purple, helios, aqua, smoke, vaseline, red, light blue with marigold overlay
Whimsey vase — clambroth, light blue with marigold overlay
Bowl, 7" – 8", round — marigold, purple, helios, smoke, amber
Fruit bowl, 11" – 12", collar base — marigold, purple, helios, smoke

## Morning Glory

This design, found only on six sizes and styles of vases, gets its name from its shape. The flared top does indeed resemble the beautiful flower for which it is named.

The miniature vase, standing only 3" to 4½" tall is most often found in marigold. Helios is a little harder to find, while purple and smoke examples are scarce. The small vase, which runs from 5" to 7" tall, exists in the same colors, as well as very rare cobalt blue example.

The standard vase ranges from 8" to 12" tall. It is most often seen in marigold, purple, and helios. Here again, smoke is scarce and cobalt blue, very rare. They have also been found in light blue with a marigold iridescent overlay. Teal examples have been reported, but I have not been able to confirm them. White and ice green examples are also rumored to exist, but again, these are not confirmed.

Two sizes of funeral vases, a 13" to 16" mid size and an impressive, large, 17" to 19" size, are also known. Both are rarely found in any color. The mid size has been reported in marigold, purple, and helios. The large funeral vase is known in marigold, purple, helios, and smoke. All are rare.

The only other version known is a jack-in-the-pulpit vase, which is found in two sizes. Some were shaped from the mold used for the standard vase, and some were made from the mid-size vase mold. These are quite plentiful in marigold. They are really very rare in purple, smoke, and emerald. The usual height is in the 6" to 9" range.

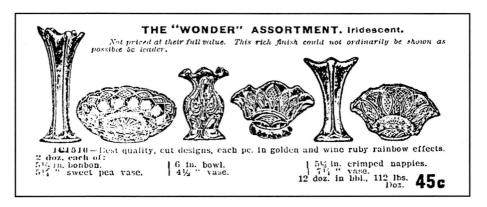

*Two styles of **Morning Glory** vases are included in this assortment from the fall 1910 Butler Brothers catalog.*

*A 6" **Morning Glory** bud vase and a Swirled Morning Glory 7" vase, both in marigold.*

*A very scarce jack-in-the-pulpit **Morning Glory** vase in smoke.*

## Shapes and Colors Known

Vase, miniature, 3" – 4½" — marigold, purple, helios, smoke
Vase, 5" – 7" — marigold, purple, helios, smoke, cobalt blue
Vase, 8" – 12" — marigold, purple, helios, smoke, cobalt blue, light blue with marigold overlay (teal, white, ice green?)
Vase, mid size, 13" – 16" — marigold purple, helios
Vase, funeral, 17" – 19" — marigold, purple, helios, smoke
Vase, jack-in-the-pulpit — marigold, purple, smoke, emerald

## Nucut #537

Starting in 1914, Imperial produced a line of several non-iridized patterns that they called their Nucut line. These designs were all of the geometric type, produced on very heavy crystal. They were often signed with the Nucut trademark. The Whirling Star and Hexagon Cane patterns, discussed elsewhere in this book, were part of this line. Also part of this Nucut line is the compote pictured here.

It stands roughly 4½" tall and is pictured in the original factory catalogs as a jelly compote. This rare compote has been found only in marigold to date, and is signed with the Nucut trademark. Other non-iridized crystal shapes are known in this pattern, but have not yet surfaced in the carnival. They likely exist, so be on the lookout for them.

*Only a few of these **NUCUT #537** jelly compotes are known.*

## Shapes and Colors Known

Jelly compote, 4½" — marigold

## Number 5

Imperial's #5, sometimes called Banded Fleur De Lis, is one of the earliest designs made by this firm. It appears in non-iridized crystal in the spring 1906 Butler Brothers catalog. The carnival version was produced very early in the carnival era, circa 1909 – 1910, and its run was apparently a very short one. Only two shapes are known and both are quite scarce.

Dome-footed, ruffled, 7" – 9" bowls are known in marigold and amber, with the amber examples especially hard to find.

A pedestal-based, 6" tall celery vase is the only other carnival shape reported. They are very scarce and have been reported only in marigold to date. No other shapes are known. It's a shame because the design would lend itself well to a four-piece table set.

*The rare marigold **Imperial's #5** celery vase.*

**Shapes and Colors Known**

Bowl, 7" – 9" — marigold, amber
Celery vase, 6" — marigold

## Octagon

Octagon is one of the most widely known and easily recognized of all the numerous Imperial geometric or near-cut patterns. It must have been an immensely popular seller, as examples of many of the known shapes are numerous on the market today. This was Imperial's #505 pattern, and to date we can document at least 23 carnival shapes. The pattern was made in an even greater variety of non-iridized crystal shapes, so other carnival shapes likely exist, but are as yet unreported.

Three sizes of pitchers exist. The most often found is the mid-size water pitcher which stands roughly 8" tall. It is quite easily found in marigold and is very rare in purple. Standing about 2" taller, the tankard pitcher is seen far less often, but marigold examples do turn up on occasion. Here again, the purple ones are very rare. A small, 6½" milk pitcher is actually quite scarce in marigold and very rare in purple.

The standard octagon tumbler rests on a ground base with no collar. It is known only in marigold and is one of the most easily found of all carnival glass tumblers. The Octagon Variation tumbler has a distinct collar base and stands about ¼" taller than the standard version. It is not found as often, but marigold examples are still reasonably plentiful. The other colors will present a challenge. This tumbler is very scarce in purple and helios. Very rare examples in aqua and olive are also known. The top ranking goes to the smoke tumbler. Only two examples have been reported to date. Surely the matching pitchers must exist for at least some of these colors, but they have not yet surfaced.

A full, four-piece table set was also made, and it is actually quite scarce and underrated, even in marigold. It is very rare in helios or purple. The butter dish is also known in a beautiful shade of aqua, so the other pieces to the set likely exist in that color.

This marigold standard-size **Octagon** water pitcher is one of the most easily found of all carnival glass pitchers. The stemmed sherbet and the punch cup are both very scarce.

Two very rare **Octagon** 5" compotes in teal and purple.

These purple **Octagon** salt and pepper shakers are extremely rare.

The marigold **Octagon** stemmed wine is easily found, but the tiny stemmed one-ounce cordial is extremely rare.

The marigold **Octagon** wine set is one of the most available of all carnival glass wine sets.

The stoppered wine decanter is another shape familiar to most collectors. It is quite easily found in marigold. The purple decanters are very rare and highly treasured. Rarer still is the helios decanter, even though it might not bring the raves that the magnificent purple examples do. I know of only a couple of examples. The matching, stemmed wines are also quite easily found in marigold. The purple ones are quite scarce, but do turn up with a little searching. Helios wines are also very scarce, but I must admit that I have seen a fair number of them over the years. Clambroth examples are quite rare. The top honors are shared by the ultra-rare aqua and white wines. Only one example of each color is known.

Other known stemware includes a tiny cordial which is extremely rare in marigold. At least one aqua example is also known. Large goblets are not too difficult to find in marigold. Very rare examples in light blue with marigold iridescent overlay also exist, as do rare amber goblets.

Bowl shapes include a berry set known in marigold, very scarce helios, and rare purple. A large, 10" – 11" bowl is also known. Most examples are of a round, deep shape, but on very rare occasion, square examples are found. It is found most often in marigold, but helios and purple examples do exist. There is some controversy surrounding one other color. Some examples have been found in a beautiful, pastel ice blue. Some feel that they are old, while others insist that they are reproductions. I have seen some of these trademarked with the IG logo, and these, of course, are new. I have also seen them unmarked. I have compared the two, and there are differences. The IG marked bowl was heavier and the molding was not as crisp. The unmarked one was lighter in weight and the molding was flawless. I am becoming convinced that at least some of these ice blue bowls are indeed old.

Another problem area concerns the toothpick holder. Old ones do exist in marigold and purple, and they are very rare. There are numerous reproductions in a wide variety of colors, so be advised.

Several other Octagon shapes exist, and all of them are rather scarce. A tall stemmed compote is known, seen most often in marigold. Very rare examples in purple are also known. Here again, this compote has been reproduced, so look for the IG trademark on the new ones. A somewhat smaller, 5" – 6" tall stemmed compote is known, and it is actually rarer than the large one. It is found most often in marigold, but very scarce teal and very rare purple examples are known. A scarce 8" pedestal-footed vase is known. It has been found in marigold and clambroth. Very rare salt and pepper shakers in marigold and purple have also surfaced. The other known shapes have all been found only in marigold. These include a scarce, one-handled nappy; a very rare stemmed sherbet; and a punch cup. While the punch cup was often marketed as a custard cup, a matching punch bowl and base has been reported to me. I have not been able to confirm it, however. I have often wondered if some of the old Octagon 10" – 11" round, deep bowls might, in reality, be the missing punch bowls. The matching base is the key here. If anyone has one, I would sure like to hear from you.

This pattern underwent considerable reproduction in the 1960s and 1970s. A wide variety of shapes were made in marigold, smoke, helios, white, purple, and red. All are signed with the IG trademark.

**Shapes and Colors Known**

Master berry bowl, 8" – 9" — marigold, purple, helios
Small berry bowl, 4" – 5" — marigold, purple, helios
Large bowl, 10" – 11" — marigold, purple, helios (ice blue?)
Water pitcher, large — marigold, purple
Water pitcher, mid size, 8" — marigold, purple
Milk pitcher — marigold, purple
Tumbler, ground base — marigold

Tumbler, collar base — marigold, purple, helios, aqua, olive, smoke
Butter dish — marigold, purple, helios, aqua
Creamer, spooner, covered sugar — marigold, purple, helios
Wine decanter — marigold, purple, helios
Stemmed wine — marigold, purple, helios, clambroth, aqua, white
Stemmed cordial — marigold, aqua
Stemmed goblet — marigold, amber, light blue with marigold overlay
Toothpick holder — marigold, purple
Vase, pedestal footed, 8" — marigold, clambroth
Large stemmed compote — marigold, purple
Compote, stemmed, 5" – 6" — marigold, purple, teal
Salt and pepper shakers — marigold, purple
Handled nappy — marigold
Stemmed sherbet — marigold
Punch cup — marigold
Punch bowl and base — (reported in marigold — unconfirmed)

## Optic and Buttons

Old Imperial factory catalogs list this as Imperial's #582 pattern. In non-iridized crystal, the design underwent a massive production spanning nearly 20 years. In fact, the catalogs list it as one of Imperial's open stock patterns. Open stock means simply that wholesalers and retailers could order any quantity or variety of the design at any given time. There was always a huge supply on hand or in production. The factory catalog illustrates 28 different shapes in non-iridized crystal.

Carnival production of Optic and Buttons was a little more limited, yet still quite extensive. To date, we can document at least 14 carnival shapes. Many of them are found with the Imperial Cross mark, and are still quite available. However, some are scarce and a few are very rare. The tiny, two-handled, pedestal-based open salt is very rare, as is its larger cousin, the similarly shaped nut cup. There are two styles of tumblers and both are very rare. One is straight sided while the other is slightly taller with a widely flared rim. Scarce items include the water pitcher, the stemmed goblet and smaller wine, and the cup and saucer.

The range of colors known in this design is very limited. A beautiful pastel clambroth is the most often seen in most shapes, followed closely by marigold. The only shapes documented in any other color are the 6" and 7½" flat plates, the stemmed compote, and the round 8"

*This assortment of **Optic and Buttons** includes a marigold cup and saucer, stemmed wine, two-piece salad set, and rose bowl. The rare stemmed compote is an unusual, delicate pastel shade of lavender.*

*This tiny **Optic and Buttons** open salt is signed with the Imperial Cross mark. It is very rare.*

bowl. The two sizes of plates are known in smoke, while the bowl and compote are known in an unusual pastel shade of lavender.

Many shapes other than those listed here were made in non-iridized crystal. Any of them could well surface in carnival. These include a full table set, four styles of cruets, water carafes, vases, salt and pepper shakers, and many others. Be on the lookout for them.

**Shapes and Colors Known**

Bowl, round, 5" — marigold, clambroth
Bowl, round, 8" — marigold, clambroth
Bowl, round, two-handled — marigold, clambroth
Rose bowl — marigold, clambroth
Water pitcher — marigold, clambroth
Tumbler, two styles — marigold, clambroth
Stemmed goblet — marigold, clambroth
Stemmed wine — marigold, clambroth
Open salt, two-handled, 5" — marigold
Cup and saucer — marigold, clambroth
Plate, 6" — marigold, clambroth, smoke
Plate, 7½" — smoke

## Optic Flute

This simple little design is often overlooked, even though it is usually found with an exceptionally brilliant iridescent lustre. The pattern consists of a row of tiny raised diamonds around the base of the exterior surface. The body of the pieces contains a faintly molded Wide Panel or Flute-like design.

Large, ruffled 8" – 9" bowls and small, 5" bowls, which make up a most attractive berry set, are the most often found shapes. Marigold, clambroth, smoke, and purple are the colors reported, with the purple examples the least often seen.

The only other shape known is a very pretty stemmed, ruffled compote, standing about 4½" tall with a diameter of 6" – 6½". Like the bowls, these are quite easily found. The only colors reported to date are marigold and clambroth, but smoke examples would come as no surprise.

*Optic Flute stemmed compote in marigold.*

**Shapes and Colors Known**

Berry set — marigold, clambroth, purple, smoke
Compote — marigold, clambroth
Spittoon, stemmed — marigold

## Oval and Round

This is one of the earlier Imperial patterns that was produced in non-iridized crystal prior to the carnival era. It is listed in the factory catalogs as Imperial's #89. The design is quite similar to that of the Three Row and Two Row vases. Even in non-iridized crystal, the factory catalog lists only berry sets and a large 10" flat plate. Those are also the only carnival shapes known, with one exception.

The berry set is comprised of an 8½" master bowl and small 4½" bowls. Most examples are ruffled, and are quite plentiful in marigold. Purple examples are really very rare, but they do exist. Helios examples have also been found. They are probably even rarer than the purple, but, as that color is not as popular with collectors, they often receive little attention. The master berry bowl has also been reported in amber.

The large 10" flat chop plate is found primarily in marigold. They are really very rare and are often underrated. I can also report one example in amber.

The only other carnival shape known is a collar-based rose bowl, shaped from the 8½" bowl mold. They have been reported only in marigold, and are not easily found.

*While marigold **Oval and Round** ruffled bowls are quite easy to find, the rose bowl shown here is quite rare.*

**Shapes and Colors Known**

Berry set — marigold, purple, helios, amber
Chop plate, 10" — marigold, amber
Rose bowl — marigold

## Pansy

One of the most widely recognized Imperial carnival patterns, Pansy is listed in the factory catalogs as Imperial's #478. This design must have been a very popular seller when it was made, for with very few exceptions almost all of the shapes and colors made can still be found with relative ease. This gives the collector a chance to own some beautifully iridized examples of Imperial carnival glass without spending a large amount of money.

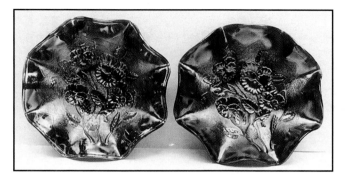

These two **Pansy** 9" bowls illustrate beautifully Imperial's different iridescent treatments. Both are on purple glass. The example on the left has the azure iridescent treatment. The bowl on the right was given the purple glaze iridescence.

This amber **Pansy** pickle dish is still quite easily found.

The iridescence on this purple **Pansy** oval dresser tray simply defies description.

One of the most available shapes is the 8" – 9½" ruffled bowl. The exterior surface carries the Imperial's Arcs pattern. They are plentiful in marigold and helios, and not really too hard to find in Imperial's beautiful purple. They are a little harder to find in amber and actually quite scarce in smoke. Lavender examples are also known and these are indeed quite rare. Rarest of all are the aqua examples. Only a few are known.

There is a second bowl shape known, and it is somewhat controversial. It is nearly flat, with a very low ruffle to the very outer edge. Some collectors consider these to be ruffled plates. My apologies to those who may call them that, but I am of the old Don Moore school of thought. If it is ruffled, it is not a true plate. I consider them to be low ruffled bowls. You call them what you wish. They are found in the same colors as the standard ruffled bowl, though they are somewhat more scarce in all of them.

Another shape familiar to most collectors is the oval pickle or relish dish, as it is sometimes called. The exterior carries a pattern called Quilted Diamonds. They are plentiful in marigold, helios, and clambroth. A fair number of amber examples turn up as well. The rare colors here are cobalt blue and ice blue. I have only heard of two or three examples of each. Imperial made very little cobalt blue and almost no ice blue at all.

A flat, oval dresser tray, shaped from the same mold as the pickle dish is one of the rarer items is this design. They have been found in marigold, purple, helios, clambroth, and amber.

They are not often seen in any color, but marigold, helios, and clambroth examples probably turn up the most. Amber is scarce and the purple ones are very rare.

Pansy is also found on a small, two-piece breakfast set, comprised of the creamer and two-handled, open sugar. These are quite easily found in marigold, clambroth, helios, and even amber. They are somewhat harder to find in purple, but a little persistence should prove fruitful. They have also been reported in a beautiful pastel shade of aqua.

The only other shape known is a round, single-handled nappy with the Quilted Diamonds exterior patterned. The handle is fashioned like a twig. They are known in marigold, purple, helios, amber, and smoke. The smoke examples are very scarce, but the other colors are all quite available.

Two of these shapes, the oval pickle dish and the one-handled nappy, were reproduced in the 1960s and 1970s. The colors made include marigold, smoke, helios, white, pink, and red. All were marked with the IG trademark.

### Shapes and Colors Known

Bowl, ruffled, 8" – 9½" — marigold, purple, helios, lavender, smoke, amber, aqua
Bowl, low ruffled, 9½" — marigold, purple, helios, smoke, lavender, amber
Oval pickle dish — marigold, purple, helios, clambroth, amber, cobalt blue, ice blue
Oval dresser tray — marigold, purple, helios, clambroth, amber
Breakfast sugar and creamer — marigold, purple, helios, amber, aqua
Handled nappy — marigold, purple, helios, clambroth, smoke, amber

## Parlor Panels

Parlor Panels is found only on vases varying in height from 4" to as much as 17". Most examples found are in the 8" to 11" size range. The squat, 4" vases are little jewels. They have been reported in marigold and purple, with both colors exhibiting a brilliant, multicolor iridescence. This size is very scarce in either color. The vases in the standard size range of 8" to 12" are most often found in marigold and purple, but even these are rather scarce. Examples in smoke are even harder to find, but well worth the effort. Helios is the rarest color in this size range. Very few examples are known. The iridescent lustre on these few helios examples is of

***Parlor Panels*** *squat vase in marigold.*

114

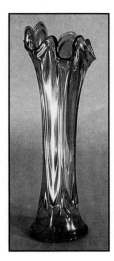

*An extremely rare honey amber **Parlor Panels** 14" vase.*

*This beautiful 7" **Parlor Panels** vase, in smoke, is very scarce.*

a brighter, richer tone than most pieces of Imperial carnival in this color. They almost bridge the gap between helios and emerald. The only other color reported to date is a pastel honey amber. It has been reported on a large 14" tall example, but I suspect that other sizes will be found in this color as well. The large 17" vase has been reported only in marigold to date, but I would not be surprised if a purple or smoke example exists.

Vases in the 6" to 8" size range are also reported in marigold, purple, and smoke.

In general, Parlor Panels vases are not easily found in any size or color. This pattern has not been reproduced.

### Shapes and Colors Known

Squat vase, 4" — marigold, purple
Vase, 5" – 7" — marigold, purple smoke
Vase, 8" – 12" — marigold, purple, smoke, helios
Vase, 12" – 14" — marigold, purple, smoke, honey amber, helios
Vase, 17" — marigold

## Pillar Flute

Many previous carnival references call this design Lustre and Clear. Pillar Flute is the original pattern name and it is listed as such in the old Imperial factory catalogs, along with the designation of Imperial's #682. Over 30 shapes were made in non-iridized crystal. About half that number are found in carnival.

Virtually all of the known carnival shapes are found primarily in marigold and clambroth. A few have also been found in smoke, and the three-piece console set is known in red.

Most of the known shapes are quite abundant and easily found. There are a few exceptions. The water set is actually quite scarce, as are the salt and pepper shakers. The smoke pieces, especially the vase, are also harder to find. The vase is pedestal footed. The compote, of course, is stemmed and the breakfast sugar and creamer are footed. All other pieces of Pillar Flute are collar based.

Carnival shapes other than those listed here are certainly possible. Many of the shapes known are found signed with the Imperial Cross mark.

*An example of the **Pillar Flute** breakfast creamer in smoke, and a marigold 8" pedestal-footed vase. The vase is still easily found, but the little creamer is scarce in smoke.*

## Shapes and Colors Known

Bowl, round, 10" — marigold, clambroth, smoke
Bowl, round, 6" — marigold, clambroth, smoke
Bowl, square, 6" — marigold, clambroth
Compote — marigold, clambroth, smoke
Console set, three piece — marigold, clambroth, smoke
Celery tray, oval, 8" — marigold, clambroth, smoke
Oval pickle dish, handled — marigold, clambroth
Plate, square, 6" — marigold, clambroth
Rose bowl — marigold, clambroth
Salt and pepper shakers — marigold, clambroth
Water pitcher — marigold, clambroth
Tumbler — marigold, clambroth
Vase, footed, 8" — marigold, clambroth, smoke

## Plain Jane

My hat's off to Marion Hartung for coming up with such an appropriate name for this pattern if, indeed, you can call it a pattern at all. Plain Jane is just that — plain, although the exterior does have a very faint Wide Panel design.

Bowls in the 7" – 9" size range are the most often encountered shapes. Most examples are ruffled and have an 18-point star molded on the underside of the collar base. They are known in marigold and smoke. The smoke examples are really quite beautiful, often showing a lovely pink and peacock blue iridescence.

A handled basket, standing 9¾" tall, is also known. Marigold and smoke are the most frequently found. Examples in white, ice green, and aqua are much harder to find. Many of these exhibit a stretch effect to the iridescence.

*Plain Jane 8" bowl in marigold.*

**Shapes and Colors Known**

Bowl, 7" – 9" — marigold, smoke
Handled basket — marigold, smoke, white, ice green, aqua

## Poinsetta

What a shame that Imperial chose to make only one shape in this beautiful pattern. It would have made a spectacular water set or table set. Milk pitchers, standing roughly 6" tall at the spout, are the only shapes known.

*The **Poinsettia** milk pitcher is easily found in marigold. Helios examples, like this one, are very scarce.*

Marigold examples abound and collectors should have little trouble in finding one. The other colors are quite another story. Helios examples are the next most often found, but even so, they are very scarce. Smoke examples are quite rare and will command a premium price. Purple Poinsettia milk pitchers are very rare and highly treasured by those fortunate enough to own an example. Everyone seems to want one and for good reason. They usually exhibit spectacular iridescence and they are well worth the effort it will take to find one. The only other color reported is a rich emerald green with iridescence that can only be described as beyond belief. Like all Imperial carnival pieces in that color, they are extremely rare and real show stoppers whenever they are shown.

**Shapes and Colors Known**

Milk pitcher — marigold, purple, helios, smoke, emerald

## Imperial's Poppy Show

Poppy Show is listed in the factory catalogs as Imperial's #488. To avoid confusion, the name Imperial's Poppy Show should be used. Northwood made a pattern of the same name, but the two designs are very different.

Imperial's Poppy Show is primarily found on large, 12" tall vases. The moldwork is outstanding and the iridescence is often quite dazzling. They are not easily found, even in marigold, the most available color. They may also be found in a lighter, pastel marigold as well as a true clambroth. Both are much harder to find than the marigold examples. Helios examples are harder still to find, but as is the case with so many Imperial patterns in this color, the popularity just isn't there. Examples in purple and smoke are extremely rare. The iridescence

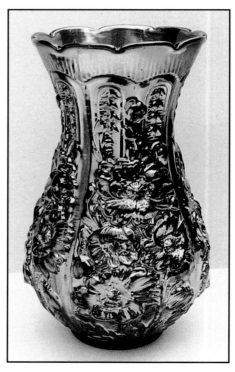

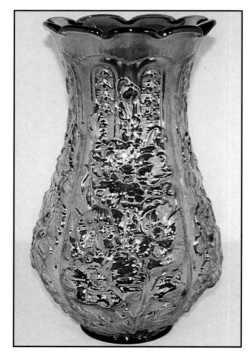

*There simply are no proper words to adequately describe the iridescence on this purple **Poppy Show** vase.*

*This helios **Poppy Show** vase exhibits the rich, silver/gold lustre that is typical for this iridescent treatment.*

on the purple vases often defies description, exhibiting a dazzling, multicolor, radium lustre. A striking pastel pink, peacock blue, and yellow iridescence highlights the beautiful smoke vases. The top spot on the rarity list is occupied by the amber Poppy Show vase. Only one example is known!

There are two other shapes known in this design. Many collectors are not aware of them. The first is a hurricane lamp. They were factory made and are of the same configuration as the vase. They rest on a metal base, and of course, they accommodate a candle. Only two examples, both in purple, are known. The other known shape is an electric table lamp, also factory made. Here again, the configuration is the same as the vase. The top has been turned or cupped inwards to accommodate the fitting plate for the electric fixture. The lamp rests on a footed, metal base. Only one example, in a rich marigold, is known!

The Poppy Show vase was reproduced in the 1960s and early 1970s. They were made in marigold, smoke, and helios. All examples bear the IG trademark.

### Shapes and Colors Known

Vase, 12" — marigold, purple, smoke, helios, clambroth, pastel marigold, amber
Hurricane lamp — purple
Table lamp, electric — marigold

## Premium

Premium is listed in the Imperial factory catalogs as Imperial's #635. Technically, the only shapes made in this design are 8½" tall candlesticks. However, they were often sold in company with an Imperial's #656 Wide Panel bowl, forming a three-piece console set. Sometimes a fourth piece, a 14" Wide Panel flat plate was also included. They are shown both ways in the factory catalog.

Premium candlesticks are still quite available in marigold and clambroth. The other colors will present a challenge. Smoke examples are very scarce and helios even more so. They are

*The marigold **Premium** candlestick.*

rarely found in purple. Amber examples are near the top of the rarity list, just below the celeste blue. Most of the examples in this rare color have the onion-skin effect of stretch iridescence. No other carnival colors have been confirmed, but I would not be surprised if others, such as red or ice green examples with stretch type iridescence, one day surfaced.

**Shapes and Colors Known**

Candlesticks, 8½" — marigold, purple, helios, amber, clambroth, smoke, celeste blue

## Propellor

This simple but effective design underwent considerable production in a variety of shapes in non-iridized crystal. The crystal version first appeared in the 1905 Butler Brothers Wholesale Catalog. Production of the carnival glass version was apparently quite limited, as only three shapes are known.

The most often encountered shape is a small, ruffled compote, standing just under 3" tall, with a diameter of about 5". Marigold examples are quite plentiful. Helios and green examples are rather scarce and the beautiful purple compotes are actually quite rare. Smoke is the rarest color here. I know of only a couple of examples.

A large, round, bowl-shaped compote is also known. It is quite rare and has been reported only in marigold to date. This compote measures 8" – 9" in diameter and stands roughly 4" tall.

The only other carnival shape known is a rare one, indeed. It is a stemmed, ruffled vase, shaped from one of the larger compote molds, that was made in non-iridized crystal. The shape is similar to a ruffled parfait, and the piece stands 7½" tall. Marigold is the only color reported. This vase is extremely rare, with relatively few examples known.

*This large 8" **Propellor** compote is very scarce.*

**Shapes and Colors Known**

Compote, small — marigold, purple, helios, smoke, green
Compote, large, 8" – 9" — marigold
Stemmed vase, 7½" — marigold

Talk about confusion! No less than five different companies in five different countries made a carnival glass version of this design. To make matters worse, all of them produced the pattern in nearly identical shapes, and all primarily in marigold. Trying to sort it all out has been a real headache. Carnival glass versions of Ranger were made by Imperial; the Crystal Glass Company of Sydney, Australia; Christales de Mexico, of Mexico; the Josef Inwald Company, of Prague, Czechoslovakia; and at least one English firm.

I now feel confident that, as far as carnival glass production is concerned, Imperial originated the design. It is listed in old Imperial factory catalogs as Imperial's #711 pattern. Imperial was known to have exported carnival glass to Europe, Central America, and Australia. How interesting it is to note that this is exactly where all of these other firms are located! Further, it is known that the carnival glass produced by these foreign firms was made from the mid 1920s through the early 1930s. That would be well after the time that Imperial exported carnival glass to these countries. It is therefore likely that the European, Australian, and Mexican versions of Ranger were copies based on the examples that Imperial sent to those countries!

Imperial factory catalogs confirm that Imperial produced the design in the following shapes: water pitcher, tumbler, breakfast creamer and sugar, sherbets, various sizes of bowls ranging from 6" to 10" in diameter, and an 8" pedestal-footed vase. The vase is listed as being available in marigold, smoke, and clambroth. All other shapes are known only in marigold.

All of these shapes were also made by virtually all of the aforementioned foreign companies. The examples made by Christales de Mexico are signed with that firm's trademark which consists of a letter M enclosed within a letter C. Without copies of factory catalogs from all of these other firms, it is virtually impossible to sort out just who made what!

**Shapes and Colors Known**
(Imperial Only)

Water pitcher, tumbler, creamer, sugar, sherbet, bowls — marigold
Vase, pedestal-footed, 8" — marigold, smoke, clambroth

*Carnival glass examples of the **Ranger** pattern are known to have been made by five different companies on three continents. The marigold tumbler shown here was definitely made by Imperial.*

Ripple is one of the most widely known and recognized carnival vase patterns, and for good reason. The variety of sizes, colors, and shapes in which the design is known is one of the most extensive in the entire carnival glass field. With a very few exceptions, the majority of the sizes and colors known in this pattern are still quite available. This makes the ripple vases a collector favorite. A most impressive collection of Ripple vases can be assembled, and without spending a small fortune.

Five different molds were used to make the Ripple vases. The difference is in the base diameter. They are as follows:

Base diameter – 2½": These have a 16-point star molded in the base. They may range in height from 4½" to 10½".

Base diameter – 2⅞": These have a 20-point star molded in the base. They range in height from 5¼" to 12¾".

Base diameter – 3⅜": These have a 20-point star in the base and range in height from 6½" to 14½".

Base diameter – 3⅞": These have a 20-point star in the base and range in height from 10½" to 16½".

Base diameter – 4¾": These have a 24-point star in the base and range in height from 11½" to 20".

Collectors also classify these vases by height into four different styles. They are squat vase, standard vase, mid-size funeral vase, and large funeral vase. The variety of colors known for each height classification varies considerably, so we will take them one at a time.

Squat vase, 4½" to 6½" — These vases were made from the first three molds listed above. They are most often found in marigold, purple, and helios. Examples in clambroth and amber also exist, but are harder to find.

*The variety of **Ripple** vase colors, shapes, and sizes is almost endless, as evidence by these beautiful assortments.*

Standard vase, 7½" to 12½" — The widest variety of colors is found in this size. Here again, examples in marigold, purple, and helios are quite easily found. Even the amber and clambroth examples turn up in fair numbers. The other colors will present a challenge. They are scarce in smoke, aqua, teal, lavender, and vaseline. White examples are very rare and cobalt blue vases, even more so. I can also confirm at least one extremely rare red example. These vases were made from the first four molds listed above.

*Two very rare **Ripple** vases. The red vase is the only confirmed example. While not in the same class, the true frosty white vase is also quite rare.*

Mid-size funeral vase, 13" to 16" — The variety of known colors is quite extensive here as well; however, this size is seen far less often than the squat or standard vases. Marigold and helios seem to be the most often found. Purple examples are seen less often, and amber examples are scarce. Clambroth is very scarce. This size is also known in light blue with a marigold iridescent overlay and a few very rare lavender examples also exist. A couple of very rare teal examples have also been reported. These were made from the third and fourth mold sizes listed above.

Large size funeral vase, 17" to 20" — Only four colors are confirmed here, and all are rarely found. Marigold and helios seem to be the most available. The magnificent purple examples are really very rare. Rarest of all is the beautiful teal. I know of only a few examples. These were made from the fifth mold size listed above.

Other colors may well exist (and likely do) for any of these sizes. The possibilities are virtually limitless.

With such a wide variety of colors known, I would certainly not rule out most any size and color combination. With so much to choose from and hunt for, you can have an awful lot of fun collecting Ripple vases!

**Shapes and Colors Known**

Squat vase, 5" – 7" — marigold, purple, helios, clambroth, amber
Standard vase, 8" – 12" — marigold, purple, helios, clambroth, amber, smoke, aqua, teal, red, blue, white, vaseline, olive

Mid-size funeral vase, 13" – 16" — Marigold, purple, helios, amber, clambroth, teal, light
    blue, lavender
Large funeral vase, 17" – 21" — Marigold, purple, helios, teal

## Robin

While most of the carnival glass producing firms made a wide array of patterns depicting
animals, Robin is the only Imperial carnival design that depicts any manner of fauna. It was
originally Imperial's #670 pattern, and it was made in an unusually limited variety of shapes
and colors.

Water pitchers are known only in marigold, usually with a good, rich, iridescent lustre.
They are not considered as rare; however, they are not that easily found, either. The matching
marigold tumblers are still reasonably available and a little patient searching will usually prove
fruitful. Tumblers are also known in smoke and these are very rare. Only a few examples are
known. No matching water pitcher in smoke have yet surfaced.

Handled mugs, the only other known shape, are also quite easily found in marigold.
Unusual examples with a marigold iridescent overlay on several different base colors are also
known. The most available of these are the light smoke with a marigold iridescent overlay.
Much rarer are the light green with marigold iridescent overlay. The most unusual of all are
the light green with a smoke iridescent overlay. True, all-over smoke examples also exist, and
these are, perhaps, the rarest color of all.

It seems strange that no other colors, such as purple or helios, have ever been found, but
such is the case.

Both the water set and the mug underwent extensive reproduction in the 1960s and 1970s
in a variety of colors, including marigold, smoke, white, red, and ice blue. Look for the superimposed IG or LIG trademark on the new pieces.

*Robin*

**Shapes and Colors Known**

Water pitcher — Marigold
Tumbler — Marigold, smoke
Mug — Marigold, marigold on smoke, smoke, marigold on light green, smoke on light
    green

The earliest documented appearance of Imperial's carnival glass in a wholesale catalog occurred in a 1910 Butler Brother issue. The small assortment offered six different Imperial pieces. The Rococo vase was one of them.

Only three carnival shapes are known in this pattern, and the variety of colors in which they may be found is also quite limited. Small, ruffled, dome-footed vases are the most familiar of these. Standing 4" – 6" tall, they are not classified as rare, but are not all that easily found, either. Marigold is the most often seen, followed closely by the smoke examples. A couple of very rare lavender examples also exist. I have heard rumors of helios vases, but all efforts to confirm them have failed.

Only one other shape is known and it exists in two sizes. A small, 5" – 6" dome-footed bowl, shaped from the same mold as the vase, is also known. Marigold and smoke are the only reported colors. A larger, 9" version of this bowl has also been reported, but only in marigold, to date. Here again, helios has been rumored to exist, but I cannot confirm this.

*The scarce **Rococo** vase, in smoke, and a rare **Rococo** 9" dome-footed bowl, in marigold.*

**Shapes and Colors Known**

Vase, 5" – 6" — marigold, smoke, lavender (helios?)
Bowl, 5" – 6" — marigold, smoke (helios?)
Bowl, 9" — marigold (helios?)

## Royalty

For many years, punch cups were the only shape reported in this geometric design. It was believed that these had been marketed individually as custard cups, and that there was no matching punch bowl and base.

In recent years, the matching punch bowl and base has indeed surfaced. They are known only in marigold and are really quite rare. Still, several examples are now known. Those fortunate enough to own one of these punch bowls may not be aware that the proper base to accompany it is the same one used for the Long Hobstar and Hobstar and Arches fruit bowl and base. It carries the Hobstar and Arches design.

A somewhat smaller, ruffled fruit bowl and base are also known. These have been reported in marigold and smoke. They employ the same base as the punch bowl, so this likely accounts for the scarcity of bases.

No other carnival shapes are known. This pattern has not been reproduced.

*An interior view of the rare **Royalty** punch bowl. The base for this punch bowl carries the Hobstar and Arches pattern.*

**Shapes and Colors Known**

Punch bowl and base — marigold
Punch cup — marigold
Fruit bowl and base — marigold, smoke

## Scroll and Flower Panels

This impressive, 10" tall vase appears in the Imperial factory catalogs as Imperial's #480 pattern. The catalog lists it as being available in three iridescent colors — nuruby, peacock, and sapphire. This presents us with an interesting situation. To date, we have only been able to document this vase in two carnival colors — marigold and purple. The color nuruby is described in the catalog as being similar to rubigold, so we know this refers to marigold. But what about peacock and sapphire? Neither color description has ever been associated with the color we call purple. Peacock has always been assumed to be the color we call smoke. Yet the description in the catalog of the color sapphire sounds a lot more like it. It is described as a "Blue-gray iridescence on crystal glass — an entirely new effect." This would tend to support my theory that the color peacock refers to the iridescent treatment, and not the base color of the glass. If so, then in this case peacock refers to purple.

Regardless, we are left with a puzzling situation. We know that marigold and purple Scroll and Flower Panels vases do exist. There must be a third color out there somewhere, and I suspect that it will prove to be smoke.

These vases are very scarce in marigold, and extremely rare in purple.

They were reproduced, in the 1960s, in marigold and smoke. The new vases were signed with the IG trademark. The new vases also have a plain bottom with a stippled, textured effect. The old vases have an impressed star in the bottom.

*The impressive **Scroll and Flower Panels** vase in marigold.*

**Shapes and Colors Known**

Vase, 10" — marigold, purple (smoke?)

## Scroll Embossed

While some collectors call this design Peacock Eye, most know it by the name used here. It was apparently a popular design when it was made, as examples in many of the known shapes and colors are found frequently today.

Ruffled bowls, in three sizes, are among the most often seen items. These ruffled bowls are usually found with the File pattern as an exterior design. The small, 4½" – 5" bowls are found frequently in purple and marigold. Somehow during the last few years, word seems to have spread that these small purple bowls are rare. How that rumor got started is a mystery to me. In the last few months alone, I've seen at least a dozen of them for sale at shows and in shops! The only color that I would consider rare are the few smoke examples known. Two other sizes of ruffled bowls with the File exterior are known. One is of the 6½" to 7½" size range and the other generally runs 8" – 9½". They are found primarily in marigold and purple, but here again, smoke is also known. On rare occasion, all three of these bowls may be found in a non-ruffled, round, deep shape.

Bowls may also be found with a plain, unpatterned exterior. Most of these are round, deep in shape, and are not ruffled. These are seen most often in marigold, helios, and, surprisingly, aqua. They are rarely seen in purple or smoke, but examples do exist. Clambroth examples have also been reported.

Perhaps the rarest of the Scroll Embossed bowls are the few known examples that have an exterior design called Hobstar and Tassels. These rare examples are of the 8" – 9" size range, and have been reported only in helios, teal, and purple to date.

The very scarce purple 9" flat plate is a real show-stopper, often exhibiting spectacular iridescence. They are real beauties and are eagerly sought. The marigold plates are not that easily found, either. Examples in aqua and helios seem to turn up far more often. A smoke example would be a real find. None have ever been reported to date. These plates all have a plain, unpatterned exterior.

Three sizes of stemmed compotes are also known. The larger ones generally have the Curved Star exterior pattern. They are found primarily in marigold and helios, but rare purple

*This scarce helios **Scroll Embossed** compote carries the Curved Star exterior pattern.*

***Scroll Embossed** 9" plate and 7" round bowl in purple.*

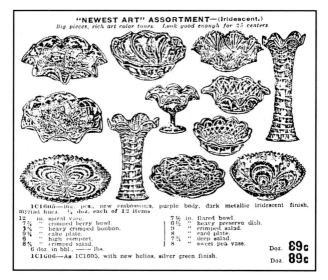

*The **Scroll Embossed** plate and bowl are part of this assortment from the mid spring 1911 Butler Brothers Wholesale catalog.*

examples are also known. The small compote has a plain exterior. These are seen most often in helios, aqua, and marigold. Purple examples are scarce. They are rarely found in amber and rarer still in olive.

A tiny, miniature compote, only about 3" tall, is very rare in any color. They have been reported in marigold, purple, and a beautiful pastel lavender.

A stemmed goblet, shaped from the small compote mold, has also been reported, but only in helios to date.

Two other shapes, a stemmed sherbet and a small nut dish, both in purple, have also been found. No other carnival shapes have been reported.

### Shapes and Colors Known

Bowl, File exterior, 4" – 5" — marigold, purple, smoke
Bowl, File exterior, 6½" – 7½" — marigold, purple, smoke
Bowl, File exterior, 8" – 9½" — marigold, purple, smoke
Bowl, plain exterior, 8" – 9" — marigold, purple, smoke, helios, aqua, clambroth
Bowl, Hobstar and Tassel exterior, 8" – 9" — purple, helios, teal
Plate, 9" — marigold, purple, helios, aqua
Compote, Curved Star exterior — marigold, purple, helios
Compote, plain exterior — marigold, purple, helios, amber, aqua, olive
Compote, miniature — marigold, purple, lavender
Goblet — Helios
Sherbet — Purple
Nut dish — Purple

## Shell
## Shell and Sand

The only difference between Shell, and Shell and Sand is the addition of a heavily stippled background on the Shell and Sand version. Otherwise, they are identical. This pattern in very seldom found and eagerly sought. Most examples exhibit magnificent iridescence.

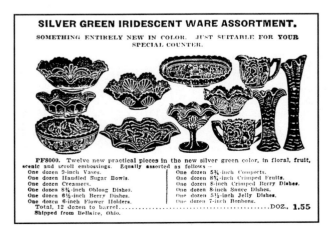

*The **Shell** bowl stands out in this assortment of helios pieces from the October 1918 Charles Broadway Rouss Wholesale catalog.*

*A beautiful **Shell** 9" plate in pastel smoke.*

Ruffled bowls, in two sizes, are the most available shape. Even so, they are relatively scarce. The smaller of these measures 6½" to 7" in diameter. They are found most often in marigold or helios. Purple examples are very scarce. Larger, 8" – 9" ruffled bowls are known in the same three colors. They are also found in smoke and amber. Both are really very rare. On rare occasion, examples in either size are found in a non-ruffled, round, deep shape.

The only other confirmed shape in carnival is the 9" flat plate. Make no mistake about it, these plates are very rare in any color. Marigold and helios examples do turn up from time to time, but still, they are really underrated as to rarity. Examples in purple and smoke are extremely rare and desirable. Often exhibiting exceptional iridescence, they are highly treasured and command very serious prices.

While a stemmed compote in this design has been rumored to exist in marigold, I have not been able to confirm it.

*This purple **Shell and Sand** 8" bowl has a stippled background, hence the name Shell and Sand.*

**Shapes and Colors Known**

Bowl, 6½" – 7" — marigold, helios, purple
Bowl, 8" – 9" — marigold, helios, purple, smoke, amber
Plate, 9" — marigold, helios, purple, smoke

## Six Sided

Imperial produced a greater variety of carnival glass candlesticks than any of their competitors. The Six Sided candlesticks are far and away one of the best and most desirable of all of them. Standing 7½" tall, these beauties are very seldom found in any color. Marigold is the most often seen color, but even these are very scarce. Examples are also known in smoke and helios. There are probably more smoke examples known than there are helios; however, the smoke will command greater attention and value. Helios is just not that popular with today's collectors. The purple Six Sided candlesticks are absolute known-outs. The iridescence is usually magnificent. They are very rare and are highly treasured by anyone fortunate enough to own a pair.

Imperial reproduced this candlestick in the 1960s, but only in non-iridized crystal.

*The **Six Sided** candlesticks, rare even in marigold.*

**Shapes and Colors Known**

Candlesticks, 7½" — marigold, purple, smoke, helios

## Smooth Panels

Smooth Panels differs from the Flute pattern in two respects. On Flute, the panels are slightly concave, and are on the exterior surface of the piece. On Smooth Panels, they are slightly convex, and are on the interior surface. The pattern is found on vases that may vary in height from 6" to as much as 12". Most examples found are generally in the 7" to 9" range. The only other known shape is a tiny rose bowl shaped from the same mold as the 4" to 5" vases. It measures 2¾" tall with a diameter of 4¼".

The only two commonly found colors in the vase shape are marigold and clambroth. Virtually all others range from scarce to extremely rare. Of these, smoke is probably the most available, followed closely by purple. Marigold on milk glass examples are very scarce, but the beautiful teal vases are even harder to find. The true, red vases are awfully close to winning the top honors, but my vote goes to a most unusual color. One example is known with a beautiful smoke iridescence over a milk glass base.

***Smooth Panels** rose bowl and 4" vase in clambroth.*

131

The only colors reported to date for the rose bowl are marigold and clambroth, but I would not be surprised if others exist. These pretty little jewels are very seldom found. In fact, I only know of a few examples.

I have not been able to document any other colors, but I would not be surprised if helios examples exist.

**Shapes and Colors Known**

Vase, 5" – 12" — marigold, purple, clambroth, smoke, marigold on milk, teal, red, smoke on milk glass

Rose bowl, small — marigold, clambroth

## Imperial's Smooth Rays

Imperial's Smooth Rays line was actually a combination of four different pattern numbers. They are listed in the factory catalogs as #M-345, #M-399, #M-422, and #M-755. A close examination of the pieces in all of these pattern numbers reveals the designs to be identical. In fact, many of the items sold in sets, like the salad set and the sundae set, are combinations of two or even three of these pattern numbers. The name Imperial's Smooth Rays should always be used in order to avoid confusion with Westmoreland's Smooth Rays pattern. The variety of shapes known is quite extensive, but the range of colors is very limited. Many of the known shapes were actually marketed as some very unique sets. Most collectors are probably not aware of this, as these pieces are often found individually. The old factory catalogs have been a big help in sorting it all out.

An eight-piece salad set is comprised of six 8" plates, a 12" plate, and a 10" round deep, straight-sided bowl. All of these items are known in marigold, clambroth, and teal.

A 9" round, flared-edge bowl and six stemmed sherbets made up a sundae set. These pieces are known in marigold and clambroth.

Seven different styles of stemware pieces are also known. They are as follows: goblets in 10 oz. and 9 oz. sizes, a 6 oz. champagne, a 4 oz. claret, stemmed wines in 3 oz. and 2 oz. sizes, and a tiny, 1 oz. cordial. All are known in marigold and clambroth. The cordial is actually very rare.

**Smooth Rays** *8" plate in marigold.*

Other known shapes include a breakfast creamer and open sugar found in marigold and clambroth. A water pitcher, tumbler, and a custard cup are also known. They have been reported only in marigold.

Some examples of Smooth Rays are found signed with the Imperial Cross mark.

**Shapes and Colors Known**

SALAD SET:
Plate, 12" — marigold, clambroth, teal
Bowl, 10", straight sided — marigold, clambroth, teal
Plate, 8" — marigold, clambroth, teal

SUNDAE SET:
Bowl, 9", flared — marigold, clambroth
Stemmed sherbet — marigold, clambroth

OTHER SHAPES:
Goblet, 10 oz. — marigold, clambroth
Goblet, 9 oz. — marigold, clambroth
Champagne, 6 oz. — Marigold, clambroth
Claret, 4 oz. — marigold, clambroth
Wine, 3 oz. — marigold, clambroth
Wine, 2 oz. — marigold, clambroth
Cordial, 1 oz. — marigold, clambroth
Custard cup — marigold
Water pitcher — marigold
Tumbler — marigold

## Snow Fancy

I'm sure that many readers will be surprised to see this pattern listed here. For many years, most carnival reference sources have credited this design to the McKee Glass Company. However, recent research findings by this writer have provided conclusive proof that it is an Imperial product. It is pictured in a 1922 Butler Brothers Wholesale catalog assortment in company with known Imperial designs. These assortments were packed at the factory of their origin, so this appearance firmly places Snow Fancy in the Imperial family.

The carnival shapes most often found are a creamer and an open sugar. This so-called open sugar is now known to be the spooner to a four-piece table set. The appearance of that covered sugar in the 1922 Butler Brothers ad confirms that this open sugar is actually the spooner. The only color reported for the creamer and spooner is marigold. Both the covered sugar and the butter dish (which obviously must exist) have not yet been reported in carnival. Sooner of later, they will likely turn up.

The only other carnival shapes known are small, 5" to 6" bowls, reported in marigold, white, purple, and helios. They are very likely part of a berry set, although no master bowl has yet surfaced.

All examples of Snow Fancy are really quite rare, even though at present they do not usually command high prices. Now that they are known to be Imperial and that the existence of a covered sugar, butter dish, and master berry bowl are virtually assured, this situation will likely change.

## Shapes and Colors Known

Creamer, spooner — marigold
Bowl, 5" – 6" — marigold, helios, white, purple

*One of four known purple **Snow Fancy** 5" bowls.*

## Soda Gold

Soda Gold seems to have come along fairly late in the carnival glass era. It appears in the April 1929 issue of the Butler Brothers Wholesale catalog, and again in the October 1930 issue, but only in a non-iridized form. In fact, it never does appear in an iridized form in any of the known Butler Brothers catalogs. This, along with the fact that virtually all known shapes are found in only the same two carnival colors, may indicate that the carnival version of the design may have been made exclusively for a specific customer. Examples are not that easily found, another indication that the design was made for a specific customer or had a relatively short production run.

*Part of the three-piece console set, this **Soda Gold** rolled-down rim console bowl is really quite rare in any color.*

*Only a few Imperial water set patterns are found in smoke, and the **Soda Gold** is a collector's favorite.*

134

Scarce water sets are found in marigold and smoke. Both colors are nearly equal in rarity, but the smoke examples seem to be the most desirable with collectors. They are handsome sets, often exhibiting a beautiful blend of pastel pink and peacock blue iridescence.

A three-piece console set, comprised of a 9" bowl, usually with a rolled-down rim, and a pair of squat, 3½" candlesticks, is also known. Here again, the colors known are marigold and smoke, with the smoke examples the hardest to find. The candlesticks actually turn up with reasonable frequency, but the rolled rim console bowl is very tough to find.

The only other carnival shapes known are salt and pepper shakers in marigold and smoke, and a large 11" – 12" chop plate, reported only in marigold. Both are very scarce.

### Shapes and Colors Known

Water pitcher, tumbler — marigold, smoke
Console bowl, rolled rim — marigold, smoke
Candlesticks, 3½" — marigold, smoke
Chop plate, 11" – 12" — marigold
Salt and pepper shakers — marigold, smoke

## Spiral

I have always had some reservations about crediting these candlesticks to Imperial. I still do. However, they have been documented in smoke, a color almost exclusive to Imperial, so I will list them here as a likely Imperial product. My doubts probably stem from the fact that most of the marigold examples I have seen had a very pale, washed-out iridescence which is just not typical of Imperial's marigold.

Apparently these 8¼" tall candlesticks were the only items produced in this pattern. I have never seen or heard of a matching centerpiece bowl or any other shapes. They are known in marigold, smoke, and green. The green examples that I have seen seem to fall somewhere between helios and emerald. They have a silver/gold iridescent sheen, but some multicolor highlights are present. These candlesticks are rather scarce and not often encountered.

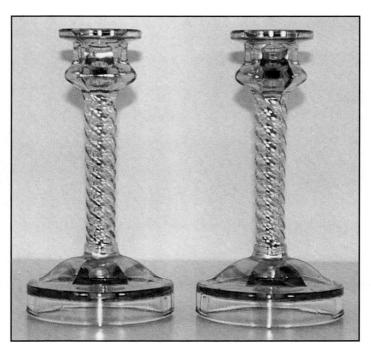

*Spiral candlesticks in a light, pastel marigold.*

Candlesticks, 8¼" — marigold, smoke, green

# Star and File

Star and File must have been one of Imperial's best sellers. At least 20 shapes are known to have been produced in carnival, and the non-iridized crystal production was even more extensive. Carnival production of the design spanned a good many years, as examples appear in the wholesale catalogs until as late as 1929. Imperial factory catalogs list this pattern as Imperial's #612.

For some unknown reason, Imperial chose to produce this design primarily in marigold. In fact, Imperial factory catalogs state that the design was available only in marigold. However, some exceptions to this are known. The large compote is found in clambroth. Very rare examples of the rose bowl are known in purple, helios, and amber. A single ice green rose bowl is also known to exist.

With virtually all other shapes known only in marigold, there would be little purpose in a lengthy, descriptive text here. There are a few noteworthy observations that will be mentioned. After that, I will simply list all the known carnival shapes, with mention of their status concerning rarity.

The most elusive item in this pattern seems to be the stemmed goblet. It is illustrated in the factory catalogs, yet no examples have ever surfaced. Keep your eyes peeled for this one, as there must be some out there somewhere.

Mention should also be made of the three tumbler sizes. The standard size tumbler is 4¼" tall. It is a little on the scarce side, yet still available. The taller, 4¾" ice tea tumbler is extremely rare. In fact, only one example is known. Equally rare is the tiny juice tumbler, which rests on a pedestal foot.

The 6½" flat plate was actually sold as an underplate to accompany the stemmed fruit salad (which we call the champagne), the sherbet, the goblet, and the tall ice tea tumbler.

Some of the more easily found pieces are the rose bowl, round and square bowls, the oval relish, the creamer and open sugar, and the sherbet.

*Marigold **Star and File** handled celery vase, wine decanter, and wines. The wine decanter is very scarce and underrated.*

*Perhaps this will give you an idea of just how tiny the little one-ounce **Star and File** cordial really is!*

**Shapes and Colors Known**

All shapes except rose bowl and large compote are known only in marigold.

Bowl, round, 7" – 8"
Bowl, square, 7" – 8"
Creamer and open sugar
Celery vase, tall, two-handled (scarce)
Stemmed compote — Marigold and clambroth known
Champagne (rare)
Water pitcher (very scarce)
Tumbler, standard, 4¼"
Tumbler, ice tea, 4¾" (extremely rare)
Juice tumbler, footed (extremely rare)
Wine decanter and stopper (scarce)
Stemmed wine
Stemmed goblet (extremely rare)
Stemmed cordial (extremely rare)
Stemmed sherbet
Oval relish, two-handled
Custard cup (scarce)
Plate, 6½"
Tall stemmed ice cream (rare)
Rose bowl — Known in marigold, purple, helios, amber, ice green. Extremely rare in all except marigold.
Nut bowl, 5" — marigold

## Star Medallion

Like its close cousin, Star and File, Star Medallion was produced in a wide variety of shapes over an extended period of time. It appeared in the wholesale catalogs well into the late 1920s. It is listed in the Imperial factory catalogs as Imperial's #671.

*The **Star Medallion** milk pitcher is abundant in marigold. The standard size tumbler is a little harder to find.*

*This clambroth **Star Medallion** celery vase is scarce.*

Perhaps the most familiar shape to most collectors is the milk pitcher. They are abundant in marigold or clambroth, but a little harder to find in smoke. Still, with a little searching, they can be had. There are two sizes of tumblers to accompany them. The standard size tumbler is 4" tall and the Star Medallions tend to be somewhat elongated in shape. The taller, 4½" lemonade tumbler has a more widely flared lip, and the Star Medallions have a much more square appearance. Both sizes are known in marigold and smoke, with the smoke examples much more difficult to find. There is no matching, full-size water pitcher. Both the milk pitcher and standard size tumbler have also been reported in helios, but both remain unconfirmed as of this writing.

Large, 9½" flat plates are also a familiar shape. They are one of the most easily found carnival plates. The clambroth examples are the most numerous, but they are also known in marigold and smoke. The smoke examples are actually quite rare. A small 6½" plate is also known in marigold and these, too, are actually rather scarce.

Other rare Star Medallion shapes include a stemmed compote, a two-handled celery vase, and a stemmed goblet. All are known in marigold and smoke, and are very seldom found.

Round and square bowls in the 6" to 7½" size range are quite easily found in marigold, clambroth, and smoke.

A small, round bowl, which rests on a slightly domed, pedestal foot, is known as well. This variation is quite scarce and has been reported only in marigold.

The only other carnival shape documented is a small punch cup. These were marketed individually as custard cups, and there is no matching punch bowl or base.

A much wider variety of Star Medallion shapes were produced in non-iridized crystal, including a full, four-piece table set, so other carnival shapes are a definite possibility.

*The **Star Medallion** goblet is one of the more difficult shapes to find in this design. The smoke example shown here is particularly scarce.*

*Another scarce **Star Medallion** shape is this little dome-footed bowl in marigold.*

### Shapes and Colors Known

Bowl, round, 6" – 7½" — marigold, clambroth, smoke
Bowl, square, 6" – 7½" — marigold, clambroth, smoke

Bowl, round, dome-footed — marigold
Plate, 6½" — marigold
Plate, 9½" — marigold, clambroth, smoke
Milk pitcher — marigold, clambroth, smoke
Standard tumbler, 4" — marigold, smoke
Lemonade tumbler, 4½" — marigold, smoke
Stemmed goblet — marigold, smoke
Stemmed compote — marigold, clambroth
Handled celery vase — marigold, smoke
Custard cup — marigold

## Star of David

While not classified as rare, Imperial's version of Star of David is certainly not plentiful in any color. It is found only on the interior of 8" – 9" ruffled bowls. The exterior surface carries the Imperial's Arcs design.

This is one of the few Imperial patterns that is most often found in purple. The iridescence is usually quite spectacular. Helios is the next most frequently seen color. Marigold examples are actually much harder to find than either of the aforementioned colors. Smoke examples top the list in rarity. Only a comparatively few are known and on these, the iridescence is a sight to behold. No other colors have been reported, but amber is a strong possibility.

For many years, I've waited patiently for a plate to show up in this pattern. I'm still waiting. None have ever been reported. Imperial made far fewer plates than most of their competitors.

*Imperial's **Star of David** bowl in purple.*

### Shapes and Colors Known

Bowl, 8" – 9" — marigold, purple, helios, smoke
Bowl, 7" – 8", round — marigold, purple

Star Spray does not appear in any of the known issues of the wholesale catalogs. This fact, combined with the limited number of shapes and colors known suggests that this design may have been produced for a specific customer, and was not offered to the general trade. It may well have been marketed exclusively by F.W. Woolworth and Company, McCrory's, or Kresge's, all of whom were big Imperial customers.

The pattern is most often seen on 7½" collar-based, shallow, round bowls. These have been reported only in marigold and smoke. They are sometimes found in a footed, metal holder. This is another indication that these pieces were made for wholesale distribution to specific customers. A quantity of these bowls were likely purchased by a metal working firm. The footed, metal holder was then manufactured to fit them and the finished bride's bowls were then marketed.

The only other carnival shape known is a 7" flat plate. To date, it has been reported only in smoke.

*These **Star Spray** bowls are sometimes found in a metal holder, making a nice little bride's bowl. This example is in smoke.*

**Shapes and Colors Known**

Bowl, round, 7½" — marigold, smoke
Bride's bowl with metal holder — marigold, smoke
Plate, 7" — smoke

# Swirl and Swirl Rib

While these two patterns do differ somewhat, they are so similar and the range of shapes and colors for each of them are so limited, that it seems only logical to list them together.

Swirl is found only on the exterior surface of 7" – 8" urn-shaped vases. The top of these vases shows a distinct lip, giving the impression that they might have contained something. It is also possible that they may have been mass produced for the florist trade. They are one of the most easily found vases in the entire carnival glass field. They are known in marigold, clambroth, smoke, and white. The white one may take a little searching.

Swirl Rib differs in that the ribs are much wider. It is found in 8" – 9" flat plates, 6" plates, a stemmed sherbet, center-handled servers, cups, saucers, candlesticks, creamers, open sugars, several sizes of bowls, and a mug. I have often seen the sherbet and the 6" plate sold in combination, and they were very likely sold that way originally. The small plate and the sherbet are seen in marigold and clambroth. All other Swirl Rib items have been reported only in marigold. The mug has been mistakenly credited to Northwood, as the design is somewhat similar to a Swirl Rib pattern made by that firm.

*Swirl vases in smoke and clambroth.*

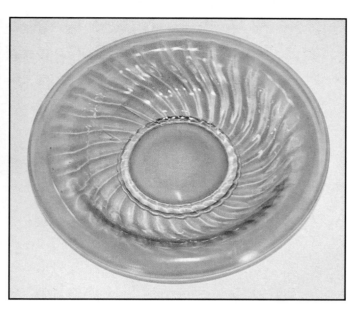

*Swirl Rib rolled rim bowl in marigold.*

**Shapes and Colors Known**

SWIRL:
Vase, 7" – 8" — marigold, clambroth, smoke, white

SWIRL RIB:
Plate, 8" – 9" — marigold
Plate, 6" — marigold, clambroth
Sherbet — marigold, clambroth
Bowls, 6" – 9" — marigold
Creamer and open sugar — marigold
Center-handled server — marigold
Cup and saucer — marigold
Candlesticks — marigold
Mug — marigold

## Thin Rib and Drape

At first glance, one might tend to think that the Thin Rib and Drape vase is nothing more than a Morning Glory vase with a drapery pattern added between the ribs. In fact, some collectors call this vase Morning Glory and Drape. The two patterns are very similar, but there are differences. The Thin Rib and Drape vase has an impressed hobstar design on the underside, while the Morning Glory has a 12-point star. The vertical ribs on Thin Rib and Drape end rather abruptly at the base while those on the Morning Glory end in rounded panels at the base.

These rather small vases range from 4" to 7" in height. Most often found are examples in the 5" to 6" range. The only colors reported are marigold, purple, helios, and cobalt blue. All are not that easily found, with the cobalt blue examples especially rare.

*Three beautiful **Thin Rib and Drape** vases in marigold, purple, and helios.*

**Shapes and Colors Known**

Vase, 4" – 7" — marigold, purple, helios, cobalt blue

## Three in One

In the old Imperial factory catalogs, this pattern carries the distinguished designation of Imperial's #1. From 1904 onward, it was made in a wide variety of non-iridized crystal shapes. The design had apparently lost much of its appeal with the buying public by the time of the carnival glass era. Imperial catalogs after about 1909 contain fewer shapes in the design, and the number of carnival shapes known is limited.

Several sizes and shapes of carnival bowls ranging from 4½" to 9" in diameter are known. Most of these are ruffled, but an occasional ice cream shaped example is found. Marigold ones are plentiful, and a fair number of examples in clambroth turn up. Helios bowls are a little tougher to locate and the beautiful smoke examples are quite scarce. As usual, the purple bowls are rarely encountered.

A very pretty little 6" – 7" flat plate is also known. They are quite rare and have been reported only in marigold.

Rarer still is the collar-based rose bowl, shaped from the 8" bowl mold. Here again, the only reported color is marigold.

The only other carnival shape known is a toothpick holder. They are very rare in marigold. Green examples are also known and there is a great deal of controversy surrounding them. Some people are convinced that they are old. I can personally assure you that a lot of them are

*This marigold* **Three In One** *rose bowl is very rare.*

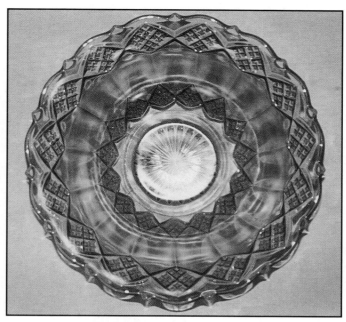

*At the opposite end of the scale is this clambroth* ***Three In One*** *6" bowl. It is very easily found.*

not! There are new examples made in 1968 that are clearly marked with the superimposed IG trademark. Green examples were made again in 1978 after Imperial had been sold to Lenox. At that time, I distinctly remember examining three of them in a giftware shop. All of them bore paper labels proclaiming them to be Imperial products, but none were trademarked in any manner. The iridescence on them was of a rich, satiny, multicolor lustre and they could have very easily passed for old carnival. I have since then seen several others on the market, some with labels intact and some without. The style of the labels is consistent with that of the ones used by Imperial in the 1970s. Of course, these labels can be easily removed.

I do not deny that some of the green Three In One toothpick holders may well be old ones. But I also will not deny that I once held new, unsigned examples in my hands, either. It does seem curious that in the early days of carnival collecting, no old green examples were documented. It has only been in recent years that the alleged old, green ones have surfaced. It has also been 18 years since the 1978 reproductions were made, more than enough time for them to start showing signs of wear. The bottom line on the green Three In One toothpick holders is simply this: we are in a very shadowy area here. Personally, I would not part with too much hard earned cash for one of them.

**Shapes and Colors Known**

Bowls, 4" – 9" — marigold, purple, helios, smoke, clambroth
Plate, 6" – 7" — marigold
Rose bowl — marigold
Toothpick holder — marigold (green?)

## Three Row

A close examination of this design reveals many similarities to the Oval and Round pattern. It could almost be classified as a variant of that design, but there are enough differences to warrant a separate classification.

Three Row is found only on the beautiful vase pictured here. This vase stands 8" tall, with a diameter of about 4½". Make no mistake about it, this is one of the rarest vases in the entire field of carnival glass. If anyone should doubt this, consider the following: the magnificent purple examples are the most often seen. I would be very surprised if more than eight or ten of them exist. Rarer still is the marigold Three Row vase. Only four or five examples are known. The top honors would have to go to the smoke Three Row vase, if a perfect one were to surface. At present, only one example is known in that color, and it is cracked. There must be a perfect one out there, somewhere.

No other colors have been reported. An example in emerald would be one of the all-time great finds. Keep your eyes peeled for these ultra-rare vases.

There is a variant of this vase called Two Row. The difference between the two is really self-explanatory. They are also extremely rare, reported only in marigold and purple. They are slightly smaller, but of the same configuration as the Three Row vase.

*While the purple **Three Row** vase is very rare, the marigold Three Row vase is extremely rare. Only three or four are known!*

**Shapes and Colors Known**

Vase, 8" — marigold, purple, smoke
Two Row Variant, 6½" – 7" — marigold, purple

## Thumbprint and Oval

While not in the same rarity class as the Three Row or Colonial Lady vases, the Thumbprint and Oval vase is till a very scarce item. These little beauties are of the same basic configuration as the Three Row vase, but stand only about 5" – 6" tall. Only two colors, marigold and purple, have been reported to date. Both are very scarce, but the marigold examples seem to be the most often encountered. The quality of the iridescence on most examples is top notch.

As the number of carnival glass collectors increases, the demand and value of these beautiful vases will surely rise. If you get a chance to buy one, I would strongly recommend that you do so.

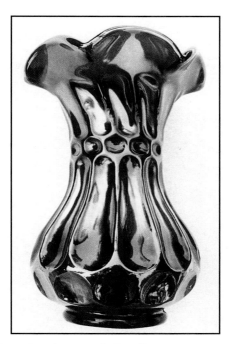

*This* **Thumbprint and Oval** *vase is yet another example of the stunning iridescence Imperial was capable of producing on their purple carnival.*

**Shapes and Colors Known**

Vase, 5" – 6" — marigold, purple

## Tiger Lily

Most of the carnival glass producing firms made some patterns of the intaglio variety. These designs are impressed rather than molded in relief. Tiger Lily, originally listed in the Imperial factory catalogs as Imperial's #484, is one of these intaglio designs.

Impressive water sets, found in a variety of colors, are the only known shapes. They are still quite available in both marigold and helios, making a handsome and affordable addition to any collection. Most of the other colors are much more difficult to find. Scarce pitchers and tumblers are known in olive and a beautiful shade of aqua. The purple water sets are a sight to behold, often exhibiting a breathtaking multicolor iridescence. They are very rare and will command a healthy price.

Tumblers are known in several other colors, including clambroth, cobalt blue, violet, and a very rare amber. In fact, only two or three amber examples are known. The cobalt blue tumblers are also extremely rare. No matching pitchers have yet been reported in any of these four colors, but they likely do exist. Keep your eyes peeled for them.

A Tiger Lily Variant tumbler also exists, but it is of European origin. It is roughly ¼" shorter than the Imperial tumbler and has a much more squat appearance. It also lacks the distinct collar base found on the Imperial version, resting instead on a flared lip which extends outward from the body. The Imperial tumbler has a 24-rayed star molded on the underside of the base, while the European version contains a hobstar-like design with a central, raised button in its base. These European copies were made in the late 1920s and early 1930s. They are known in marigold and blue. A matching pitcher has also been reported.

This water set has been reproduced, but all examples are clearly trademarked. Ice blue sets were made in 1969, and white sets in the early 1970s. They were marked with the IG trademark. Pink sets were made in 1978 and were marked with the LIG trademark. So none of these reproductions should pose any problem to collectors. In fact, they have now become highly collectible in their own right.

*In both iridescent quality and base glass color, this beautiful **Tiger Lily** water pitcher and tumbler nearly bridges the gap between helios and emerald.*

*Along with the Lustre Rose Variant water set, the **Tiger Lily** water set was featured in this ad from the October 1918 Charles Broadway Rouss Wholesale catalog.*

**Shapes and Colors Known**

Water pitcher — marigold, purple, helios, aqua, olive
Tumbler — marigold, purple, helios, aqua, olive, violet, clambroth, cobalt blue, amber
Tiger Lily Variant (European) — marigold, blue

## Tree Bark

I have some reservations about crediting this pattern to Imperial. There is virtually no concrete evidence to firmly place it in the Imperial family. I have always leaned towards Jenkins or possibly the Indiana Glass Company as the likely producer. A few tantalizing bits of information suggest that the design could have been made by the Diamond Glass Company. Still, the general consensus among most collectors is that it is Imperial, so until something substantial that proves otherwise comes along, I will list it here as a possible Imperial creation.

Tree Bark came along very late in the carnival glass era. It did not appear in the wholesale catalogs until 1927.

The marigold tankard water sets must have been made by the tens of thousands and been very popular with the buying public. Today, they are by far the most commonly seen water set in the entire field of carnival glass. They were offered in the wholesale catalogs either with a matching cover for the pitcher or without the cover. The covers likely became casualties of time and use, as they are seldom found today.

What will come as a surprise to most collectors is the fact that marigold is not the only color known in this water set. Very rare examples are known in a beautiful shade of aqua. I can personally vouch for the existence of at least one other color as well. Nearly 25 years ago, in my early days of collecting (and before I knew any better), I actually held in my hands a purple Tree Bark tankard pitcher. I distinctly remember that it was at the famous Norton Flea Market in Massachusetts, and that the pitcher had a price tag of $30.00 on it. Now, that was a lot of money for such a common item as a piece of Tree Bark. At that time, you could purchase a marigold example just about anywhere for around $5.00 or so. Having no conception as to the actual rarity of what I held in my hands, I put it down and walked away. To this day, I have never seen another! So I can assure you that at least one purple Tree Bark pitcher does exist. Where is it?

Tumblers are, of course, very common in marigold and they do exist in aqua as well. I have never seen a purple tumbler, but I'm sure that they must exist.

A second style of Tree Bark pitcher also exists. This version is mold-blown, slightly bulous and ovoid in shape, and has a separately applied, reeded handle. The same cover used on the tankard pitcher also fits this one. Marigold is the only color reported and this version of the pitcher is actually quite scarce.

Tree Bark is also found on large and small round berry bowls and a 7" – 8" flat plate. Marigold is the only reported color. The only other shapes known are two styles of vases, and candlesticks standing roughly 7" tall. One of these vases, often called a pickle jar, stands roughly 7" tall and is slightly ovoid in shape. The other is cone shaped and rests on a domed foot. Both are reported only in marigold. The candlesticks are known only in marigold.

*This marigold **Tree Bark** ovoid-shaped pitcher is seen far less often than the tankard version.*

*The **Tree Bark** tankard water set was featured in the April 1929 Butler Brothers catalog.*

**Shapes and Colors Known**

Tankard pitcher — marigold, aqua, purple
Ovoid pitcher, applied handle — marigold
Tumbler — marigold, aqua (purple?)
Vase, ovoid shape — marigold
Berry set — marigold
Plate, 7" – 8" — marigold
Plate, 7" – 8" — marigold
Vase, cone shape — marigold
Candlesticks, 7" — marigold

## Tulip and Cane

One of the earlier Imperial designs, Tulip and Cane, is listed in the factory catalogs as Imperial's #9. The pattern underwent a fairly extensive production in non-iridized crystal, but the carnival production was quite limited. Only five carnival shapes are known and four of these are found only in marigold.

A small, dome-footed bowl, which some collectors classify as a compote, is the most frequently found shape. They are known in marigold and smoke. While not considered rare, they are not that easily found, but a little persistent searching will probably pay off.

The other four shapes all fall into the stemware category. All are found only in marigold. In fact, an early factory catalog lists marigold as the only available color. The easiest to find of these shapes is the eight ounce goblet, but even they are quite scarce. Two sizes of stemmed wines, a three-ounce and a tiny 1½-ounce size, are also known, and both are very rare. I would classify the smaller of the two as small enough to be considered a cordial. It is the rarest of the two sizes. The fourth shape is a four-ounce claret, and it is extremely rare. Only a relative few are known.

The large eight-ounce goblet was reproduced in 1970 in a color called aurora jewels. This is similar to cobalt blue, but with a somewhat lighter tone and an electric iridescent effect. They were marked with the IG trademark.

*Tulip and Cane claret, goblet, wine, and cordial.*

### Shapes and Colors Known

Bowl, dome footed — marigold, smoke
Goblet, 8 oz. — marigold
Claret, 4 oz. — marigold
Wine, 3 oz. — marigold
Wine, 1½ oz. (cordial) — marigold
Vase, whimsey — marigold

## Twins

Twins is one of the most familiar geometric designs to emerge from the Imperial factory. In marigold, huge quantities of the pattern were apparently produced over a period of many years. It must have been very popular with the buying public, as marigold examples are abundant today in all known shapes.

Large 9" – 10" ruffled bowls and small 5" – 6" counterparts make up an attractive berry set. They are quite easily found in marigold. Examples are also known in helios and smoke.

The are actually very rare in either color. The smoke examples are especially beautiful with their pastel pink, yellow, and peacock blue iridescent highlights.

A two-piece, ruffled fruit bowl and base was also made. These have been found only in marigold, and examples are still quite plentiful.

The large, master berry bowl was apparently supplied in quantity to one of the many metal working firms. They are occasionally found in a silver-plated, metal holder, forming a most attractive bride's bowl. They have been reported only in marigold.

No other carnival shapes have been reported. However, a wider variety of shapes, including a water pitcher, were made in non-iridized crystal. None have turned up in carnival glass . . . yet!

*Twins fruit bowl and base in marigold. This is without a doubt the most easily found of all carnival two-piece fruit bowls.*

### Shapes and Colors Known

Berry bowl, 9" – 10" — marigold, helios, smoke
Berry bowl, 5" – 6" — marigold, helios, smoke
Fruit bowl and base — marigold
Bride's bowl, in metal holder — marigold

## Two-Handled

Two-Handled is one of several Imperial designs that bridges the gap between carnival glass and stretch glass. Some examples exhibit a rich carnival lustre. Some have the onion-skin effect of stretch glass and some have a combination of the two. Originally, the pattern was called Grecian.

The most often seen shapes are vases in the 7" – 8" height range, but even these are very scarce. They are known in four shapes. The most commonly seen of these stands 7" tall with a rolled down top rim. The second version stands 8" tall and is cone shaped. An 8" tall version, with the top flared out into a fan shape, is much harder to find. The fourth shape is that of a jack-in-the-pulpit, and also stands 8" tall. Three colors are known, with marigold being the easiest to find. Examples in smoke and white are also known. The smoke ones seem to be the most desirable of the two with most collectors.

A variant, sometimes called Two-Handled Swirl, is also known. This version of the vase has a swirled interior design. It has been found only in the 8" fan-shaped vase and the 8" cone-shaped version. It has been reported only in marigold and smoke.

The only other shape known is a most unique one that is shown here for the very first time. It is in the shape of a center-handled server, but as you can see, the center handle is actually a candlestick. The piece measures 10" in diameter and stands 8" tall. The iridescence shades from a marigold lustre to a clear, onion-skin stretch effect on the base. I know of only

 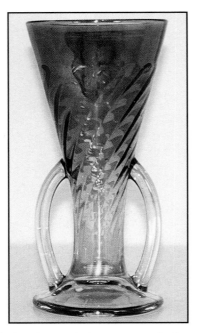

*Both the marigold **Two-Handled** jack-in-the-pulpit vase and the* ***Two-Handled*** *swirl vase in smoke are very scarce items.*

*The rare **Two-Handled** candlestick server. Only two examples have been reported.*

150

two examples, and both are owned by the same family. Reportedly, they were purchased many years ago by a family member. At that time, they were being sold under the name of Christmas Candlesticks.

The vase mold was revived in the 1930s and 1940s for production in non-iridized, etched crystal.

**Shapes and Colors Known**

Vase, 7" – 8", four shapes — marigold, smoke, white
Vase, 8", Swirl interior — marigold, smoke
Candlestick/server — marigold

## Imperial's Vintage

Imperial factory catalogs actually illustrate this design as part of the Imperial's Grape line. It bears the same pattern designation #473. However, the pattern does have several differences and most collectors have always known it as Imperial's Vintage.

This pattern is found only on the exterior surface of large, center-handled servers, with a diameter that varies from 9" to 12". The center handle is forked at the top and patterned like a grapevine branch. The edge of the server may be flat, like a plate, or turned up, like an ice cream shaped bowl. The flat version was sold as a sandwich server, while the other was advertised as a fruit dish. Both first appeared in a 1927 Butler Brothers Wholesale catalog, a rather late entry in the carnival glass field.

Both shapes may be found in marigold, clambroth, and smoke. All three colors are still quite easily found, so they must have been a popular seller. The quality of the iridescence on most examples is excellent.

*This Imperial's **Vintage** center-handled server in smoke is actually part of the Imperial's Grape pattern line.*

**Shapes and Colors Known**

Center-handled server, either shape — marigold, clambroth, smoke

151

Listed in the old factory catalogs as Imperial's #698, the carnival glass version of this design has been found in 15 different shapes to date. The molds were revived in the 1930s for production in non-iridized crystal and colored glass. The non-iridized version appears in the catalogs as Imperial's Monticello line.

The range of colors known is a curious one. Ten of the shapes are known only in marigold and clambroth. Two are known in marigold, clambroth, and teal. Two are known only in marigold and one is known only in clambroth. No other carnival colors have ever been confirmed.

One of the most available shapes is the punch bowl and base. They are frequently found in marigold and clambroth, but rare teal examples also exist. The punch cups are known in marigold and clambroth. Teal cups must surely exist, but have not been confirmed as of this writing.

The 10" tall handled basket is also easily found in marigold and clambroth. Here again, the teal examples are much harder to find.

With the exception of the 7" to 9" bowls, which are often found in marigold and clambroth, all of the other known carnival shapes are not easily found. This is especially true of the water sets. The impressive tankard pitchers, known in marigold and clambroth, are very scarce. The matching tumblers are downright rare. There are two sizes of these. The standard tumbler rests on a collar base, and is known in marigold and clambroth. The Waffle Block Variant tumbler lacks the collar base, resting on a ground bottom. Only one example, in clambroth, is known.

Other rare carnival shapes include a 6" flat plate, a collar-based rose bowl, a stemmed parfait, a 10" vase, and an open sugar and matching creamer. All of these are known in marigold and clambroth. An unusually large whimsey spittoon, shaped from the punch bowl top, is also known in marigold. The only other carnival shapes reported are salt and pepper shakers, found only in marigold to date.

Over 40 different shapes were made in non-iridized crystal. It is very possible, and in fact quite probable, that some of these will eventually turn up in carnival.

*The clambroth **Waffle Block** handled basket is one of the more easily found items in this pattern. The tankard water pitcher in marigold is rarely found.*

Bowl, 7" – 9" — marigold, clambroth
Bowl, 7" – 9", square — marigold
Plate, 6" — marigold, clambroth
Rose bowl — marigold, clambroth
Vase, 10" — marigold, clambroth
Stemmed parfait — marigold, clambroth
Sugar and creamer — marigold, clambroth
Punch bowl and base — marigold, clambroth, teal
Punch cup — marigold, clambroth
Handled basket, 10" — marigold, clambroth, teal
Water pitcher — marigold, clambroth
Tumbler, collar base — marigold, clambroth
Tumbler, variant, ground bottom — clambroth
Whimsey spittoon — marigold
Salt and pepper shakers — marigold

# Waffle and Hobstar

Even if it were not listed in the old Imperial factory catalogs, we would surely recognize this as an Imperial pattern. The design of the tall, 13" basket is quite typical of Imperial. The rope-patterned handle was used on many of Imperial's baskets. The pattern is very similar to Waffle Block. The only real difference is the addition of the narrow bands of hobstars along the top and bottom portions of the pattern. An identical vertical band runs down the side.

This is without question the rarest of Imperial's carnival glass baskets. Relatively few examples are known, and marigold is the only color reported to date. I would not be too surprised if clambroth and smoke examples exist. Though neither color has been reported, most of Imperial's baskets are known in those colors.

**Shapes and Colors Known**

Handled basket, 13" — marigold

*The marigold **Waffle and Hobstar** basket is probably the most difficult to find of all Imperial carnival baskets.*

## Wheels

Very little is known about this Imperial pattern. Few collectors even realize that it exists. The design does not appear in any of the surviving, old Imperial factory catalogs. However, the geometric design on the underside of the collar base appears on other known Imperial patterns, so there seems little doubt that Wheels is an Imperial product.

Wheels has been reported only on collar-based, round 8" – 9" bowls. The only color reported is marigold, and only a few of these bowls have surfaced.

***Wheels*** *9" bowl in marigold.*

**Shapes and Colors Known**

Bowl, 8" – 9" — marigold

## Whirling Star

Whirling Star was Imperial's #555 pattern. Originally part of Imperial's Nucut line, it was primarily produced in non-iridized crystal. However, on rare occasion, an iridized example turns up.

Known carnival shapes include ruffled bowls, stemmed compotes, and an impressive banquet punch set. The ruffled bowls are of the 9" – 11" size range and have been reported only in marigold. The stemmed compotes are found in marigold and have been reported in helios. The massive banquet punch set has been reported only in marigold, and is quite rare.

A word of caution here: this punch set was extensively reproduced in the late 1960s and early 1970s. These new sets were marked with the IG trademark. The trademark was worked into the pattern, slightly up the side of the bowl, and away from the collar base. It may be difficult to find. Some of these punch bowls were made into lamps. The punch bowl base served as the lamp base and the huge punch bowl was inverted to form the shade.

*Only one old example of the **Whirling Star** punch bowl and base has been reported, and this is the only known photo of it.*

**Shapes and Colors Known**

Bowl, ruffled, 9" – 11" — marigold
Stemmed compote — marigold (helios?)
Punch bowl and base — marigold
Punch cup — marigold

## Wide Panel

Imperial's Wide Panel actually consists of items from several different pattern numbers. These include Imperial's #645, #647, and #6569 lines. Why these items were given different pattern numbers in the Imperial factory catalogs remains a mystery. There is virtually no difference in pattern configuration between them.

The only true Wide Panel shapes are two sizes of bowls and three sizes of plates. All of these were often combined and marketed as salad sets and centerpiece sets. The salad set consisted of a 9" bowl, an 11" underplate, and six 8" plates. All of these pieces are known in marigold, white, red, clambroth, celeste blue, and teal, all often with stretch effect to the iridescence. The small plates have also been reported in pink stretch.

***Wide Panel** 12" bowl in smoke.*

The centerpiece set consisted of a large 12" bowl and an even larger 14" underplate. These were often marketed with the premium candlesticks as a four piece set. They are known in marigold, clambroth, and smoke.

These are the only items that should correctly be called Imperial's Wide Panel. Most are easily found in marigold and clambroth. The other colors are rare.

**Shapes and Colors Known**

SALAD SET:
Bowl, 9" — marigold, white, red, clambroth, celeste blue, teal
Plate, 11" — marigold, white, red, clambroth, celeste blue, teal
Plate, 8" — marigold, white red, clambroth, celeste blue, teal, pink

CENTERPIECE SET:
Bowl, 12" — marigold, clambroth, smoke
Plate, 14" — marigold, clambroth, smoke

## Windmill

Windmill is one of the most widely known of all Imperial carnival glass patterns. It is listed in the Imperial factory catalogs as Imperial's #514. While we often tend to think that the pattern was made in an extensive variety of shapes, in reality, only eight old carnival shapes are known. It is the wide variety of colors in which many of these shapes are known that probably accounts for this.

One of the most familiar of the shapes is the water set. They are still readily available in marigold, and even the helios examples still turn up from time to time. The magnificently iridized purple sets are another story. The tumblers turn up with reasonable frequency, but

*This **Windmill** milk pitcher and dresser tray are both good examples of Imperial's purple glaze iridescent treatment. Both are also very scarce items, especially the milk pitcher.*

the water pitchers are very rare and highly treasured. Rarer still are the emerald water pitchers and tumblers. I have heard of only a few examples of each. As rare as these are, they are nearly eclipsed by the cobalt blue water pitchers. Here again, only a few are known.

Tumblers are known in several other colors, all of which must be classified as very rare to extremely rare. In the very rare category are the smoke and cobalt blue tumblers. The extremely rare tumblers include olive, teal, aqua, and a beautiful pastel lavender. No matching water pitchers have yet surfaced in any of these four colors. They may well have been made, so be on the look our for them.

A smaller, one-pint milk pitcher was also made. They are actually a little harder to find than the water pitcher, but do turn up in marigold. The other colors are tough, but helios is found on occasion. Clambroth examples are known, but seldom found. The only other colors reported are smoke and purple. Both are very rare.

There are three styles and shapes of windmill bowls. Of these, the collar-based, 8" – 9" ruffled bowl is found in the widest variety of colors. Marigold examples are easily found, and a fair number of helios bowls are seen. Clambroth is a little tougher and the purple bowls are scarce, but do turn up. Smoke examples are also quite scarce and I would consider the aqua examples as rare. Two of the rarest colors are the beautiful emerald bowls and the very unusual marigold on milk glass examples. Only a few of each are known. Small 4" – 5 ruffled bowls are seen far less often. They are known in marigold, helios, purple, a very scarce smoke, and a rare emerald. Some round, deep, non-ruffled examples are also known.

Three-footed, ruffled 8" – 9" bowls are found in a somewhat more limited range of colors. They are most often found in marigold and helios. Smoke examples are quite scarce and the purple ones, rarely seen. The marigold on milk glass examples are the rarest of all, with relatively few known.

A variant of the footed bowl also exists. This version rests on short, stubby, hexagonal feet, and carries a version of the Floral and Optic design as an exterior pattern. Many collectors refer to this version as Double Dutch. These are most often found in marigold, but examples also exist in helios, emerald, purple, smoke, and amber. Of these, the purple and emerald examples are the least often found. The smoke examples are also quite scarce.

Oval pickle or relish dishes were also made. They are most often found in marigold and helios. Scarce aqua examples are known and, as usual, the purple examples are rather rare. The only other color reported is a beautiful pastel lavender. The same mold was used to make a flat, oval dresser tray. These are very scarce in any color. Helios seems to be the most frequently found, followed very closely by marigold. They are also known in aqua and the purple examples are rarely found.

From the early 1960s through the early 1980s, virtually all of these shapes were reproduced. All were marked with the IG, LIG, or ALIG trademarks. These reproductions were made in marigold, smoke, purple, helios, meadow green, red, aurora jewels (electric blue), and quite possibly others. Imperial also made new Windmill water sets in marigold with the oval windmill panel frosted. These were made in 1966, and again in 1972. Today, the Summit Art Glass Company owns many of the Windmill molds. New carnival Windmill pieces from this company are now on the market.

Colors include red, pink, vaseline, blue, and green. They are marked with the letter S in a circle.

**Shapes and Colors Known**

Water pitcher — marigold, purple, helios, emerald, smoke, cobalt blue
Milk pitcher — marigold, purple, helios, clambroth, smoke
Tumbler — marigold, purple, helios, emerald, smoke, aqua, teal, lavender, olive, cobalt blue

Bowl, collar base, 8" – 9" — marigold, purple, helios, emerald, smoke, clambroth, marigold on milk, aqua

Bowl, 4" – 5" — marigold, purple, helios, emerald, smoke

Bowl, footed, 8" – 9" — marigold, purple, helios, marigold on milk, smoke

Bowl, footed, Double Dutch Variant — marigold, purple, helios, emerald, amber, smoke

Oval pickle dish — marigold, purple, helios, aqua, lavender

Oval dresser tray — marigold, purple, helios, aqua

## Zippered Heart

It is certainly a mystery why more carnival shapes have not appeared in this impressive design. Zippered Heart is listed in the old Imperial factory catalogs as Imperial's #292 pattern. Twenty-one different shapes are illustrated in non-iridized crystal. Only five carnival shapes are known. The range of colors known is also very limited. Virtually all of the carnival shapes are very rare in any color.

The ruffled berry set, comprised of a large 9" – 10" bowl and smaller 5" counterparts, are the most available shapes, but even these are rarely found. Purple and marigold are the only colors reported.

*This extremely rare **Zippered Heart** vase stands 5" tall. Only a very few examples are known.*

***Zippered Heart** small berry bowl in purple.*

The absolutely magnificent queen's vase is 9½" to 10" tall, and rests on a sawtoothed edged, pedestal foot. These extremely rare vases are known only in purple and a stunning emerald. Only a few of each are known and they are among the most highly prized vases in the entire field of carnival glass.

A giant rose bowl, shaped from the same mold, is also known. The top is turned in, and it has been reported only in emerald to date. Actually, the Imperial factory catalog lists this shape, in non-iridized crystal, as a punch bowl. And indeed, a punch cup was made in crystal. None have been reported in carnival.

A small, 5" tall version of this rose bowl is the only other carnival shape known. Only a few examples are known in marigold.

Surely other carnival shapes will one day be found. Shapes known in non-iridized crystal include a water set, several varieties of vases and compotes, punch sets, bon-bons, and a four-piece table set. The batter dish to this set is most unusual. The base is two handled. Watch for any of these shapes in carnival. They may well exist.

### Shapes and Colors Known

Bowl, 9" – 10" — marigold, purple
Bowl, 5" — marigold, purple
Queen's vase — purple, emerald
Giant rose bowl — emerald
Rose bowl, 5" — marigold
Vase, 5" — marigold

## Zipper Loop

Kerosene lamps, in four styles, are the only known carnival shapes in this design. They are quite common in non-iridized crystal, but carnival examples are not easily found in any style or color. In both quantity and color variety, the production of these lamps was apparently quite limited. The only carnival colors reported for all styles are a good, rich marigold and a beautiful smoke.

Two sizes of tall, stemmed lamps are the most frequently seen styles, but bear in mind that even these are very scarce. Standing roughly 8" and 9½" to 10" tall, both sizes are found most often in marigold, but smoke examples do exist. There is also a shorter stemmed lamp of roughly 6" – 7" in height. This version has a much more squat appearance than its taller counterparts, and is found far less often.

There are two styles of finger or hand lamps. One stands roughly 5¼" tall and rests on a domed pedestal base. The other version stands roughly 4" tall. Both versions have round, doughnut-type handles. They are really very rare, far more so than the taller stemmed versions. Again, marigold and smoke are the only colors reported, with smoke the least often seen.

The 8" medium-size stemmed lamp was reproduced in the 1960s and 1970s in both marigold and smoke. They are trademarked with the IG logo. It is found on the underside of the stemmed base about halfway up the inside surface. It may be difficult to see, but can usually be felt. I have not heard of any reproductions of the other styles.

### Shapes and Colors Known

Stemmed lamp, squat, 6" – 7" — marigold, smoke
Stemmed lamp, medium, 8" — marigold, smoke
Stemmed lamp, large, 9½" – 10" — marigold, smoke
Hand lamp, pedestal base, 5¼" — marigold, smoke
Hand lamp, pedestal base, 4" — marigold, smoke

*Zipper Loop* medium-size stemmed lamps in marigold and smoke, shown here with the large stemmed lamp in marigold.

The **Zipper Loop** hand lamp, shown here in marigold, is probably the rarest of all the Zipper Loop lamp sizes.

# IMPERIAL'S CARNIVAL GLASS LIGHT SHADES

Imperial produced a greater variety of carnival glass electric and gas light shades than did any of the other carnival glass producing firms. Fortunately, an entire 20-page factory catalog, devoted exclusively to Imperial light shades, has survived the years. It provides us with valuable information concerning the production of their carnival glass shades.

The first page of the catalog provides descriptions of three iridescent colors in which these shades were produced. They are listed as Pearl Iridescent colors, under the names Pearl White, Pearl Green, and Pearl Ruby. These colors are those that we know as white, helios, and marigold. At some later point, amber must have been added to the line as well. It is not listed in the catalog, but examples of Imperial carnival shades do exist in that color.

There are two basic styles of Imperial carnival light shades; gas and electric. Gas shades are the larger of the two. The fitting collar has a diameter of from 6" to 7". The electric shades are much smaller, with a fitting collar of about 2¼" in diameter, and a shade diameter of from 3½" to 4½". The production of these shades occurred at a time when much of the country was in the process of converting from gas to electric lighting. Therefore, you will find the greatest variety of patterns in the electric shades.

To date, we can attribute at least 14 patterns of carnival shades to Imperial. Some are found in both gas and electric styles, and some only in electric. Some of them can be found with the Nuart trademark molded in block letters around the fitting collar.

The following list contains all of the patterns, styles, and colors known for Imperial's carnival light shades. The numbers in parenthesis are the original factory catalog numbers, where known.

August Flower (#486C) — Known only in the electric style and reported in marigold and helios. Rare in helios.

Buzz Saw — Found in both gas and electric styles. Known in marigold, helios, and amber. All are quite rare.

Colonial — Found only in the electric style. Reported in marigold and amber. Very scarce.

Diamond Block (#699C) — Same design as the Diamond Block pattern shown elsewhere in this book. Reported only in marigold, in the electric style.

Etched Greek Key — This shade has an etched Greek Key border and is known only in the electric style. It is found in marigold and helios, both with a satin frosted finish. Rare.

Fine Crosshatch (#430C) — Previously unlisted. This pattern is comprised of an extremely fine lined plaid design. This effect is produced by the fine horizontal ribbing of the interior surface and the fine vertical ribbing on the exterior surface. It is known in marigold and helios, in both gas and electric styles. Especially rare in helios.

Imperial's Grape (#473C) — Same design as the Imperial's Grape pattern shown else where in this book. Reported only in the electric style, in marigold.

Leaf Garden — Known in both gas and electric styles. Colors include white and a frosted, satin marigold.

Nuart Daisy — Usually signed Nuart. Reported in marigold, in both gas and electric styles.

Nuart Drape — The pattern and shape is reminiscent of an artichoke. It is signed Nuart and is known only in the electric style. Frosted, satin marigold is the only color reported.

Nuart Four Panels (#S 56½) — A square electric shade signed Nuart. Reported only in white.

Nuart Plain — Absolutely plain and unpatterned. They are signed Nuart, and reported only in marigold in the electric style.

Nuart Stippled — Sometimes called Clear Pillars, these are signed Nuart. Six clear, raised pillars separate panels of heavily textured stippling. Known in marigold only in the electric style.

Mayflower (#474C) — The gas and electric shade version of Imperial's 474 pattern. These shades lack the Nearcut design, but the Intaglio flower is the same. Reported in marigold and helios.

Primrose Panels — Found only in the electric style in a frosted, satin marigold.

Starlyte — Known in both gas and electric styles, this design consists of two raised stars against a paneled, stippled background. Known in marigold and helios. Helios is extremely rare.

Torch and Wreath (#49½) — Found in both styles, this design consists of a flaming torch and laurel wreaths. It is sometimes called Olympic. It is known only in marigold. This shade is one of the very few that have been reproduced.

Imperial also produced a tremendous variety of gas and electric shades in etched designs. The patterns consist of Floral, Grape, Leaf, Rococo, and geometric etchings in an almost endless variety of motifs. They are far too numerous to document here, but carnival glass versions of many of these shades likely exist.

No. 486C electric shade
2¼-inch holder
Packed 12 dozen in barrel
Per dozen, $0.45

No. 486C gas shade
4-inch holder
Packed 5 dozen in barrel
Per dozen, $0.70

**August Flower**

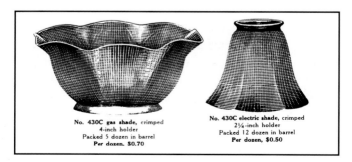

No. 430C gas shade, crimped
4-inch holder
Packed 5 dozen in barrel
Per dozen, $0.70

No. 430C electric shade, crimped
2¼-inch holder
Packed 12 dozen in barrel
Per dozen, $0.50

**Fine Crosshatch**

**No. 474C electric shade**
2¼-inch holder
Packed 12 dozen in barrel
**Per dozen, $0.45**

**No. 474C gas shade**
4-inch holder
Packed 5 dozen in barrel
**Per dozen, $0.70**

*Mayflower*

**No. 49½ electric shade**
Mould frosted all over
2¼-inch holder
Packed 12 dozen in barrel
**Per dozen, $0.50**

**No. 49½ gas shade**
Mould frosted all over
4-inch holder
Packed 5 dozen in barrel
**Per dozen, $0.75**

*Torch and Wreath*

*Nuart Stippled (Clear Pillars)*　　　　*Primrose Panels*

# BIBLIOGRAPHY

American Carnival Glass Association Newsletters, various issues, 1974 – 1994.

Archer, Douglas, and Margaret. *Imperial Glass*, factory catalog reprints.
     Paducah, KY: Collector Books, 1978.

Burns Auction Service. Auction Catalogs, 1984 – 1995.

Burns, Carl O. *The Collector's Guide to Northwood's Carnival Glass*. Gas City, IN:
     LW Books, 1994.

Butler Brothers Wholesale Catalogs, various issues, 1904 – 1932.

Charles Broadway Rouss Wholesale Catalogs, various issues, 1912 – 1919.

Edwards, Bill. *Imperial Carnival Glass — The Early Years*. Paducah, KY: Collector Books, 1980.

_____. *Rarities in Carnival Glass*. Paducah, KY: Collector Books, 1978.

_____. *The Standard Encyclopedia of Carnival Glass* 2nd Edition. Paducah, KY:
     Collector Books, 1988.

Florence, Gene. *The Collector's Encyclopedia of Depression Glass*, Eleventh Edition. Paducah, KY:
     Collector Books, 1994.

_____. *Collectible Glassware from the 40s, 50s, 60s. . .*, Second Edition. Paducah, KY: Collector
     Books, 1994.

Freeman, Larry. *Iridescent Glass*. Watkins Glen, NY: Century House, 1956.

Greguire, Helen D. *Carnival In Lights*. Published by Helen Greguire, 1975.

Hand, Sherman. *Colors in Carnival Glass*, Books 1 – 4. Published by Sherman Hand, 1972.

Hartung, Marion T. *Carnival Glass Pattern Books*, Volumes 1 – 10, 1964 – 1973.
     Now published by the Heart of America Carnival Glass Association.

Heacock, William. *Collecting Glass*, Volumes 1 – 3. Marietta, OH:
     Antique Publications, 1984 – 1986

_____. *Pattern Glass Preview*, Volumes 1 – 6, Marietta, OH:
     Antique Publications, 1980 – 1981.

_____. *The Glass Collector*, Volumes 1 – 6. Marietta, OH:
     Antique Publications, 1982 – 1983.

Heart of America Carnival Glass Association: *Carnival Glass Pattern Notebook*.

Heart of America Carnival Glass Association Newsletters, various issues, 1973 – 1995.

Imperial Glass Company Factory Catalogs, various issues and dates, 1962 – 1980.

Imperial Glass — House of Americana Glassware Catalog #66A, Reprinted by the National Imperial Glass Collectors Society, 1991.

Lincoln-Land Carnival Glass Club News, various issues, 1985 – 1995.

Moore, Donald E. *Carnival Glass — A Collection of Writings*. Published by the Heart of America Carnival Glass Association.

Moore, Donald E. *The Complete Guide to Carnival Glass Rarities*. Published by Donald E. Moore.

Moore, Donald E. *The Shape of Things in Carnival Glass*. Published by Donald E. Moore, 1975.

Mordini, Tom and Sharon. *Carnival Glass Auction Price Reports*, 1984 – 1994.

Olsen, O. Joe. *Carnival Glass News and Views*, various issues, 1973 – 1981.

_____. *Carnival Glass Tumbler and Mug News*, various issues, 1978 – 1979.

Owens, Richard E. *Carnival Glass Tumblers*. Published by Richard E. Owens, 1973.

Rainbow Review Glass Journal: Published by Ben and Barbara Shaeffer, Costa Mesa, CA. Various issues, 1972 – 1978.

Resnik, John D. *The Encyclopedia of Carnival Glass Lettered Pieces*. Published by John D. Resnik, 1989.

Ross, Richard and Wilma. *Imperial Glass*. Wallace-Homestead Book Company, 1971.

Russell, E. Ward. *National Carnival Glass News*, various issues, 1973 – 1975.

Shaeffer, Barbara. *Glass Review Magazine*, various issues, 1979 – 1986.

The Imperial Glass Collector's Glasszette, Journal of the National Imperial Glass Collectors Society, various issues, 1990 – 1994.

Uambraco, Kitty and Russell. *Iridescent Stretch Glass*. Berkeley, CA: Cembura and Avery Publishers, 1972.

*Wholesale Catalogs Selling Carnival*. Published by the San Diego County Carnival Glass Club and the Southern California Carnival Glass Club, 1994.

Wiggins, Berry. *Stretch In Color*. Orange, VA: Green Publishers Inc., 1971.

# PRICE GUIDE TO IMPERIAL'S CARNIVAL GLASS 1998 – 1999

Since the publication of this value guide in 1996, there have been exciting developments in the field of Imperial carnival glass. No longer shunned as a "second-class citizen," Imperial's carnival glass has gained a new appreciation from and popularity with collectors. With this has come some astounding value increases, especially in the areas of plates, water pitchers, and many of the rarer and more desirable vases. This is particularly true with regards to purple pieces. Prices realized at the carnival glass auctions for many items in these areas have nearly tripled! Likewise, there have been some dramatic gains with regards to Imperial's emerald green. Prices for helios, smoke, and amber pieces have remained relatively stable, with a few significant gains in some areas. These price changes are all reflected in this updated guide.

In a few instances there have been some significantly lower prices realized. In most cases these are the result of an unusually large number of some of these items being sold or made available for sale within a relatively short period of time. This should not be a cause for alarm. It is part of the normal cycle of collecting, and in time, values will rebound.

Price guides are a necessary evil. They are one of the most misunderstood and misused forms of printed matter in the entire field of collectibles. They only encourage speculation for financial gain and drive prices to unrealistic levels. Collecting for enjoyment and the love of the glass itself becomes secondary, and in time will become lost altogether. However, the rapid expansion of interest in carnival glass over the last few years demands that some form of value guide be included here.

The values listed in this guide represent actual prices paid at auctions, antique shops. antique shows, and private sales. These values are for items in *perfect condition*, with *top quality iridescence.* Items with average or below average iridescence will generally bring from 25 to 40% less. Items with damage will often bring only a small fraction of the values listed here. Purchasing damaged items is purely a judgement call of the part of the buyer.

Prices realized at auctions can be very deceiving. If you have just two people in attendance who have both made up their minds that they simply *have* to have that piece, it is likely that the price realized for that item will be pushed to a very unrealistic level. We are starting to see this happen more and more frequently at the carnival glass auctions. Auction prices must therefore be considered with a healthy dose of salt. Remember, the following should only be used as a general guide. Values are not written in stone. They can vary greatly from one area of the country to another. Both the author and the publisher can assume no responsibility for any transactions made as a result of using this guide.

The following abbreviations have been used for the colors listed in the column OTHERS:

M/Bl — Light blue with marigold overlay  
Cel Bl — Celeste Blue  
IB — Ice blue  
IG — Ice green  
Lav — Lavender  
Lime — Lime green  
MMG — Marigold on milk glass  
PM — Pastel marigold  

R — Red  
SMG — Smoke on milk glass  
Vas — Vaseline  
Vio — Violet  
W — White  
M/Gr — Marigold on light green  
Aq — Aqua  

166

| | MARI | PURPLE | HELIOS | EMERALD | COBALT | SMOKE | AMBER | CLAM | OTHERS |
|---|---|---|---|---|---|---|---|---|---|
| **ACANTHUS** | | | | | | | | | |
| Bowl, 8" – 9" | $50.00 | $135.00 | $80.00 | $250.00 | $275.00 | $95.00 | | $65.00 | Aq, $165.00 |
| Plate, 10" | 170.00 | | | | | 275.00 | | 175.00 | |
| **ARCS** | | | | | | | | | |
| Exterior Pattern | | | | | | | | | |
| **BALLOONS** | | | | | | | | | |
| Center-handled Server | 48.00 | | | | | 65.00 | | | |
| Compote | 65.00 | | | | | 85.00 | | | |
| Perfume Atomizer | 75.00 | | | | | 85.00 | | | |
| Vase, 6½", ovoid | 75.00 | | | | | 100.00 | | | |
| Vase, 7½", corset | 90.00 | | | | | 120.00 | | | |
| Vase, 9½", corset | 100.00 | | | | | 125.00 | | | |
| Vase, 9", cylindrical | 100.00 | | | | | 125.00 | | | |
| **BANDED RIBS** | | | | | | | | | |
| Water Pitcher | 80.00 | | | | | | | | |
| Tumbler | 18.00 | | | | | | | | |
| **BEADED ACANTHUS** | | | | | | | | | |
| Milk Pitcher | 225.00 | | | | | 375.00 | | | |
| **BEADED BULLSEYE** | | | | | | | | | |
| Vase, squat, 6" – 7½" | 75.00 | 175.00 | 75.00 | | | | | | |
| Vase, 8" – 11" | 90.00 | 150.00 | 55.00 | 200.00 | 350.00 | 175.00 | 250.00 | | Lime, 175.00 |
| Vase, 12" – 14" | 100.00 | 185.00 | 65.00 | 250.00 | | | 275.00 | | |
| **BELLAIRE SOUVENIR** | | | | | | | | | |
| Bowl, 7" | 165.00 | | | | | | | | |
| **BROKEN ARCHES** | | | | | | | | | |
| Bowl, 8" – 9" | 40.00 | 100.00 | | | | | | | |
| Punch Bowl and Base | 550.00 | 1,100.00 | | | | | | | |
| Punch Cup | 30.00 | 50.00 | | | | | | | |
| **CHATELAINE** | | | | | | | | | |
| Water Pitcher | | 1,600.00 | | | | | | | |
| Tumbler | | 300.00 | | | | | | | |
| **CHESTERFIELD (#600)** | | | | | | | | | |
| Candlesticks, pair | 50.00 | | | | | 90.00 | | 40.00 | |
| Compote, sm. 5" – 6" | 20.00 | | | | | 40.00 | | 15.00 | W, 50.00 R, 175.00 Teal, 75.00 |
| Compote, lg., 11" – 12" | 40.00 | | | | | 75.00 | | 30.00 | W, 65.00 R, 250.00 Cel Bl, 100.00 |
| Lemonade Mug | 45.00 | | | | | | | | |
| Open Salt | 100.00 | | | | | | | | |
| Rose bowl | 45.00 | | | | | 75.00 | | 35.00 | W, 100.00 |
| Sherbet | 15.00 | | | | | 35.00 | | 10.00 | W, 35.00 R, 100.00 Teal, 50.00 |
| Stemmed rose bowl | 50.00 | | | | | | | 50.00 | W, 90.00 |
| Toothpick, handled | 250.00 | | | | | | | | |
| Water Pitcher, covered | 145.00 | | | | | | | | R, 500.00 W, 225.00 Cel Bl, 325.00 |

| | MARI | PURPLE | HELIOS | EMERALD | COBALT | SMOKE | AMBER | CLAM | OTHERS |
|---|---|---|---|---|---|---|---|---|---|
| **CHESTERFIELD (#600), cont.** | | | | | | | | | |
| Tumbler | 40.00 | | | | | | | | R, 200.00 |
| | | | | | | | | | W, 75.00 |
| | | | | | | | | | Cel Bl, 100.00 |
| **CHRYSANTHEMUM** | | | | | | | | | |
| Chop Plate, 10½" | 700.00 | 1,700.00 | 2,000.00 | 3,500.00 | 5,000.00 | 2,000.00 | 2,500.00 | | W, 1,000.00 |
| **COBBLESTONES** | | | | | | | | | |
| Bowl, 8" – 9½" | 125.00 | 325.00 | 140.00 | | 500.00 | | 250.00 | | |
| Plate, 9" | | 1,500.00 | | | | | | | |
| **COLONIAL** | | | | | | | | | |
| Buttermilk Goblet | 30.00 | | | | | | | | |
| Candlesticks, pair | 45.00 | 100.00 | | | | | 80.00 | 40.00 | |
| Creamer or Sugar | 30.00 | | | | | | | | |
| Lemonade Mug | 45.00 | | | | | | | | |
| **COLONIAL LADY** | | | | | | | | | |
| Vase, corset shape | 800.00 | 700.00 | | | | | | | |
| Vase, 8" flared top | 475.00 | | | | | | | | |
| **COLUMBIA** | | | | | | | | | |
| Bowl, 7" – 8" | 35.00 | | | | | | | | |
| Compote, stemmed | 55.00 | 125.00 | | | | 90.00 | | 45.00 | |
| Plate, 7½" – 9" | 100.00 | | | | | | | 90.00 | |
| Rose bowl | 475.00 | | | | | | | | |
| Vase, 5" – 7" | 45.00 | 225.00 | 80.00 | | | 150.00 | | | |
| **CONE AND TIE** | | | | | | | | | |
| Tumbler | | 550.00 | | | | | | | |
| **CORN BOTTLE** | | | | | | | | | |
| Bottle, 5" | 275.00 | | 200.00 | | | 375.00 | | | |
| **CRABCLAW** | | | | | | | | | |
| Berry Bowl, lg. | 40.00 | 150.00 | 65.00 | 125 | | 125.00 | | 50.00 | |
| Berry Bowl, sm. | 15.00 | 45.00 | 20.00 | | | 100.00 | | 10.00 | |
| Bowl, ice cream | | | | | | | | 75.00 | |
| Decanters (cruet) | 450.00 | | | | | | | | |
| Water Pitcher | 195.00 | | | | | | | | |
| Tumbler | 40.00 | | | | | | | | |
| **CRACKLE (Tree of Life)** | | | | | | | | | |
| Bowl, 5" – 6" | 5.00 | 15.00 | 20.00 | | | | | | |
| Bowl, 8" – 9" | 10.00 | 25.00 | 25.00 | | | | | | |
| Candlesticks, pair | 35.00 | | | | | | | | |
| Candy Jar, covered | 20.00 | 40.00 | | | | | | | |
| Car Vase | 25.00 | | | | | | | | |
| Plate, 6" – 8" | 10.00 | 30.00 | 35.00 | | | | | | |
| Salt and Pepper, pair | 85.00 | | | | | | | | M/Bl, 100.00 |
| Wall Vase | 25.00 | | | | | | | | |
| Water Pitcher | 50.00 | | | | | | | | |
| Tumbler | 10.00 | | | | | | | | |
| **CRUCIFIX** | | | | | | | | | |
| Candlesticks, pair | 1,800.00 | | | | | | | | |

| | MARI | PURPLE | HELIOS | EMERALD | COBALT | SMOKE | AMBER | CLAM | OTHERS |
|---|---|---|---|---|---|---|---|---|---|
| **CURVER STAR** | | | | | | | | | |
| Compote, Ext. Pattern | 45.00 | 150.00 | 70.00 | 150.00 | | | | | Lime, 150.00 |
| **DAISY BASKET** | | | | | | | | | |
| Handled Basket | 50.00 | | | | | 100.00 | | 45.00 | |
| **DIAMOND BLOCK** | | | | | | | | | |
| Candlesticks, pair | 75.00 | | | | | | | 50.00 | |
| Compote | 60.00 | | | | | | | 45.00 | |
| Milk Pitcher | 100.00 | | | | | | | 90.00 | |
| Rose bowl | 75.00 | | | | | | | 65.00 | |
| Tumbler, juice size | 30.00 | | | | | | | 30.00 | |
| Vase, 8" – 9", ped. ftd. | 75.00 | | | | | 125.00 | | 65.00 | |
| Vase, 12", cylindrical | 200.00 | | | | | | | | |
| **DIAMOND LACE** | | | | | | | | | |
| Bowl, 8" – 9" | 35.00 | 100.00 | 60.00 | | | | | | |
| Bowl, 5" | 18.00 | 40.00 | 25.00 | | | | | | |
| Water Pitcher | | 400.00 | | | | | | | |
| Tumbler | 200.00 | 50.00 | | | | | | | |
| Whimsey Rose bowl | 1,800.00 | | | | | | | | |
| **DIAMOND RING** | | | | | | | | | |
| Bowl, 8" – 9" | 30.00 | 100.00 | 55.00 | | | 50.00 | | | |
| Bowl, 5" | 12.00 | 40.00 | 20.00 | | | 30.00 | | | |
| Rose bowl | 125.00 | 400.00 | | | | 300.00 | | | |
| **DIAMOND AND SUNBURST** | | | | | | | | | |
| Goblet | 100.00 | | | | | | | | |
| Wine Decanter | 150.00 | 500.00 | | | | | | | |
| Wine, stemmed | 30.00 | 60.00 | | | | | | | |
| **DOUBLE SCROLL** | | | | | | | | | |
| Candlesticks, pair | 60.00 | | | | | 100.00 | | 50.00 | R, 375.00 Teal, 225.00 W, 350.00 |
| Console Bowl, oval | 75.00 | | | | | 150.00 | | 50.00 | R, 375.00 Teal, 225.00 |
| Punch Cup | 25.00 | | | | | | | | |
| **ETCHED LUSTRE** | | | | | | | | | |
| Vase, 6" | 50.00 | | | | | 75.00 | | 50.00 | |
| Vase, 8" – 12" | 80.00 | | | | | 100.00 | | 50.00 | |
| **FANCY FLOWERS** | | | | | | | | | |
| Bowl, 8" – 9", ped. ftd. | 125.00 | | 175.00 | | | | | | |
| **FASHION** | | | | | | | | | |
| Bowl, 9", ruffled | 30.00 | | | | | 125.00 | | | |
| Bowl, 9", ice cream | 70.00 | | | | | 175.00 | | 80.00 | |
| Breakfast Creamer | 60.00 | 225.00 | 150.00 | 250.00 | | 100.00 | | | |
| Breakfast Sugar | 60.00 | 225.00 | 150.00 | 250.00 | | 100.00 | | | |
| Compote, Large | | | | | | 600.00 | | | |
| Punch Bowl and Base | 125.00 | 2,500.00 | | | | 1,500.00 | | | R, 5,000.00 |
| Punch Cup | 15.00 | 65.00 | | | | 50.00 | | | R, 525.00 |
| Rose bowl | 200.00 | 1,500.00 | 350.00 | | | | | | |
| Water Pitcher | 145.00 | 1,500.00 | | | | 500.00 | | | |
| Tumbler | 35.00 | 350.00 | | | | 100.00 | | | |

|  | MARI | PURPLE | HELIOS | EMERALD | COBALT | SMOKE | AMBER | CLAM | OTHERS |
|---|---|---|---|---|---|---|---|---|---|
| **FIELDFLOWER** | | | | | | | | | |
| Milk Pitcher | 250.00 | 475.00 | 300.00 | | | | | 250.00 | |
| Water Pitcher | 175.00 | 650.00 | 225.00 | | 1,500.00 | 750 | 400.00 | | Aq, 550.00 |
| Tumbler | 35.00 | 135.00 | 45.00 | | | | 75.00 | | R, 1,500.00 |
| | | | | | | | | | Vio, 250.00 |
| | | | | | | | | | Olive, 100.00 |
| **FILE** | | | | | | | | | |
| Bowls, 7" – 9" | 45.00 | | | | | | | | |
| Butter Dish | 200.00 | | | | | | | | |
| Creamer or Spooner | 50.00 | | | | | | | | |
| Covered Sugar | 75.00 | | | | | | | | |
| Chop Plate, 11" | 175.00 | | | | | | | | |
| Water Pitcher | 750.00 | | | | | | | | |
| Tumbler | 100.00 | | | | | | | | |
| Whimsey Vase | 475.00 | | | | | | | | |
| **FLORAL AND OPTIC** | | | | | | | | | |
| Bowl, 8" – 9", footed | 40.00 | 300.00 | | | | 100.00 | | 30.00 | R, 325.00 |
| | | | | | | | | | Teal, 150.00 |
| | | | | | | | | | MMG, 135.00 |
| Cake Plate, 11", footed | 75.00 | | | | | | | 65.00 | R, 300.00 |
| | | | | | | | | | Teal, 165.00 |
| | | | | | | | | | W, 100.00 |
| Rose bowl, footed | 65.00 | | | | | 125.00 | | 60.00 | R, 300.00 |
| | | | | | | | | | Teal, 175.00 |
| | | | | | | | | | MMG, 150.00 |
| **FLUTE (#700)** | | | | | | | | | |
| Berry Bowl, lg. | 65.00 | 135.00 | | | | | | | |
| Berry Bowl, sm. | 20.00 | 35.00 | | | | | | | |
| Bowl, 7" – 8", md. sz. | 45.00 | | | 100.00 | | | | | |
| Celery Vase | 200.00 | 375.00 | | | | | | | |
| Creamer or Sugar | 40.00 | 80.00 | | | | | | | |
| Punch Bowl and Base | 350.00 | 1,10.00 | 350.00 | 850.00 | | | | | |
| Punch Cup | 30.00 | 90.00 | 35.00 | 65.00 | | | | | |
| Tootchpick Holder | 65.00 | 85.00 | 75.00 | 100.00 | 275.00 | | | | Vas, 175.00 |
| | | | | | | | | | Aq, 200.00 |
| Vase, 7", flared | 85.00 | | | | 450.00 | | | | |
| Water Pitcher | 300.00 | 900.00 | 425.00 | | 1,200.00 | | | | |
| Tumbler #1 | 45.00 | 90.00 | | | | | | | |
| Tumbler #2 | | 100.00 | | | | | | | |
| Tumbler #3 | 45.00 | 90.00 | 75.00 | | 325.00 | 250.00 | | 40.00 | Aq, 300.00 |
| **FLUTE AND CANE** | | | | | | | | | |
| Bowl, 4½" – 7½" | 30.00 | | | | | | | | |
| Champagne | 95.00 | | | | | | | | |
| Compote | 95.00 | | | | | | | | |
| Cordial, stemmed | 500.00 | | | | | | | | |
| Cup and Saucer | 200.00 | | | | | | | | |
| Creamer or Sugar | 55.00 | | | | | | | | |
| Goblet, stemmed | 65.00 | | | | | | | | |
| Milk Pitcher | 160.00 | | | | | | | | |

| | MARI | PURPLE | HELIOS | EMERALD | COBALT | SMOKE | AMBER | CLAM | OTHERS |
|---|---|---|---|---|---|---|---|---|---|
| **FLUTE AND CANE, cont.** | | | | | | | | | |
| Plate, 6" | 100.00 | | | | | | | | |
| Sherbet, stemmed | 50.00 | | | | | | | | |
| Water Pitcher | 325.00 | | | | | | | | |
| Tumbler, 9 oz. | 550.00 | | | | | | | | |
| Tumbler, 12 oz. | 550.00 | | | | | | | | |
| Wine, stemmed | 175.00 | | | | | | | | |
| **FOUR-SEVENTY-FOUR** | | | | | | | | | |
| Bowl, 8" – 9" | 75.00 | | | | | | | | |
| Compote | 175.00 | 350.00 | | | | | | | |
| Cordial, stemmed | 500.00 | 750.00 | | | | | | | |
| Goblet, stemmed | 50.00 | 125.00 | 65.00 | | | | | | |
| Milk Pitcher | 200.00 | 1,500.00 | 225.00 | 650.00 | | | | | Lav, 700.00 / Olive, 375.00 |
| Pitcher, mid sz. | 325.00 | 3,000.00 | | | | | | | |
| Punch Bowl and Base | 225.00 | 4,000.00 | 425.00 | 3,500.00 | | 2,500.00 | | | Aq, 1,500.00 |
| Punch Cup | 20.00 | 75.00 | 35.00 | 100.00 | | 75.00 | | | Aq, 50.00 / Olive, 45.00 |
| Sherbet, stemmed | 85.00 | | | | | | | | |
| Water Pitcher | 175.00 | 5,000.00 | 475.00 | 4,000.00 | | | | | Olive, 750.00 |
| Tumbler | 35.00 | 300.00 | 75.00 | 250.00 | 275.00 | | | | Vio, 175.00 / Teal, 150.00 |
| Wine, stemmed | 150.00 | | | | | | | | |
| Vase, 7" – 8", ped. ftd. | 575.00 | | | | | | | | R, 3,500.00 |
| Vase, 10", ped. ftd. | 1,100.00 | | | | | | | | |
| Vase, 14", ped. ftd. | 1,400.00 | 12,000.00 | 1,000.00 | 10,000.00 | | | | | |
| **FREEFOLD** | | | | | | | | | |
| Vase, 7" – 14" | 28.00 | 75.00 | 50.00 | 100.00 | | 95.00 | | 25.00 | White, 125.00 / Lav, 45.00 |
| **FROSTED BLOCK** | | | | | | | | | |
| Bowl, 5" – 7", round | 25.00 | | | | | | | 20.00 | W, 35.00 |
| Bowl, 8" – 9", round | 30.00 | | | | | | | 25.00 | W, 40.00 |
| Bowl, 7" – 8", square | 35.00 | | | | | | | 30.00 | W, 45.00 |
| Compote, stemmed | 45.00 | | | | | | | 40.00 | W, 65.00 |
| Creamer or Sugar | 30.00 | | | | | | | 25.00 | W, 50.00 |
| Milk Pitcher | 125.00 | | | | | | | 100.00 | |
| Pickle Dish, oval | 40.00 | | | | | | | 35.00 | W, 55.00 |
| Plate, 9½", round | 75.00 | | | | | | | 60.00 | W, 100.00 |
| Plate, 7½", round | 85.00 | | | | | 200.00 | | 75.00 | |
| Plate, 7½", square | 100.00 | | | | | | | 80.00 | W, 125.00 |
| Rose bowl, small | 100.00 | | | | | | | 65.00 | W, 100.00 |
| Rose bowl, large | 130.00 | | | | | | | 75.00 | W, 100.00 |
| Vase, 6", ped. ftd. | | | | | | 150.00 | | 75.00 | |
| **GOTHIC ARCHES** | | | | | | | | | |
| Vase, 10" – 12" | 135.00 | | | | | 400.00 | | | |
| Vase, 14" – 18" | 375.00 | | | | | | | | |
| **HATTIE** | | | | | | | | | |
| Bowl, 8", round | 40.00 | 135.00 | 75.00 | | | 120.00 | 135.00 | | |
| Bowl, 8" – 9", ruffled | 45.00 | 165.00 | 90.00 | | | 135.00 | | | |
| Chop Plate, 10" – 11" | 1,000.00 | 2,400.00 | 450.00 | | | | 4,500.00 | 750.00 | |

| | MARI | PURPLE | HELIOS | EMERALD | COBALT | SMOKE | AMBER | CLAM | OTHERS |
|---|---|---|---|---|---|---|---|---|---|
| **HATTIE, cont.** | | | | | | | | | |
| Rose bowl | 350.00 | 2,500.00 | | | | | 425.00 | | |
| **HEAVY DIAMOND** | | | | | | | | | |
| Bowl, 10" | 50.00 | | | | | | | | |
| Compote | 50.00 | | 75.00 | | | | | | |
| Creamer or Sugar | 35.00 | | | | | | | | |
| Vase, 6" – 7", ped. ftd. | 100.00 | | 125.00 | | | 150.00 | | 75.00 | |
| **HEAVY GRAPE** | | | | | | | | | |
| Bowl, 5" – 6" | 25.00 | 40.00 | 30.00 | 50.00 | | 125.00 | 35.00 | 40.00 | M/Bl, 45.00 |
| Bowl, 7" – 8" | 30.00 | 55.00 | 35.00 | 100.00 | | 150.00 | 45.00 | 40.00 | |
| Bowl, 9" – 10" | 50.00 | 225.00 | 100.00 | 275.00 | 400.00 | 225.00 | 175.00 | | M/Bl, 100.00 |
| Nappy, handled | 25.00 | 75.00 | 30.00 | 85.00 | | | | 20.00 | Olive, 50.00 |
| Plate, 6" | 600.00 | | | | | | | | |
| Plate, 7" – 8" | 100.00 | 135.00 | 65.00 | 150.00 | | 400.00 | 265.00 | 80.00 | Vas, 250.00 |
| | | | | | | | | | Lime, 225.00 |
| | | | | | | | | | Teal, 175.00 |
| Chop Plate, 11" – 12" | 200.00 | 525.00 | 225.00 | 750.00 | | 2,500.00 | 400.00 | | W, 550.00 |
| | | | | | | | | | IG, 700.00 |
| Punch Bowl and Base | 425.00 | 1,450.00 | 550.00 | 2,000.00 | | | 800.00 | | |
| Punch Cup | 50.00 | 100.00 | 65.00 | 125.00 | | | 50.00 | | |
| **HEAVY GRAPE VARIANT** | | | | | | | | | |
| Plate, 8" | 100.00 | | | | | | | | |
| **HERRINGBONE AND BEADED OVAL** | | | | | | | | | |
| Compote | 175.00 | | | | | | | | |
| **HEXAGON AND CANE** | | | | | | | | | |
| Covered Sugar | 200.00 | | | | | | | | |
| **HOBNAIL SODA GOLD** | | | | | | | | | |
| Salt and Pepper, pair | 150.00 | | | | | | | | |
| Spittoon | 50.00 | | 80.00 | | | | 90.00 | | W, 100.00 |
| **HOBSTAR** | | | | | | | | | |
| Bowl, 5" – 7" | 20.00 | 55.00 | | | | | | | |
| Bowl, 8" – 10" | 30.00 | 100.00 | | | | | | | |
| Bride's Bowl/Holder | 100.00 | | | | | | | | |
| Butter Dish | 90.00 | 200.00 | 100.00 | 250.00 | | | | | |
| Creamer or Spooner | 30.00 | 55.00 | 35.00 | 75.00 | | | | | |
| Covered Sugar | 40.00 | 75.00 | 45.00 | 100.00 | | | | | |
| Compote | 75.00 | | | | | | | | |
| Cookie Jar, covered | 80.00 | 200.00 | | | | | | | |
| Milk Jar, covered | 80.00 | | | | | | | | |
| Pickle Castor | 400.00 | | | | | | | | |
| Punch Bowl and Base | 350.00 | | | 650.00 | | | | | |
| Punch Cup | 40.00 | | | 75.00 | | | | | |
| **HOBSTAR AND ARCHES** | | | | | | | | | |
| Bowl, 8½" – 9½" | 40.00 | 125.00 | 75.00 | | | 125.00 | | | |
| Fruit Bowl and Base | 100.00 | 325.00 | 175.00 | | | 200.00 | | | |
| **HOBSTAR AND TASSELS** | | | | | | | | | |
| Bowl, 8" – 9" Ext. Pat. | | 225.00 | 150.00 | | | | | | Teal, 275.00 |
| **HOBSTAR FLOWER** | | | | | | | | | |
| Compote | 125.00 | 150.00 | 135.00 | 200.00 | | 225.00 | | | Lav, 165.00 |

| | MARI | PURPLE | HELIOS | EMERALD | COBALT | SMOKE | AMBER | CLAM | OTHERS |
|---|---|---|---|---|---|---|---|---|---|
| **HOFFMAN HOUSE** | | | | | | | | | |
| Goblet, stemmed | | | | | | | 100.00 | | |
| **HOMESTEAD** | | | | | | | | | |
| Chop Plate, 10½" | 650.00 | 1,750.00 | 2,200.00 | 4,000.00 | 7,000.00 | 2,000.00 | 2,500.00 | 500.00 | Olive, 1,200.00 |
| | | | | | | | | | W, 800.00 |
| **IMPERIAL BASKET** | | | | | | | | | |
| Handled Basket | 125.00 | | | | | 200.00 | | | MMG, 475.00 |
| **IMPERIAL PAPERWEIGHT** | | | | | | | | | |
| Paperweight | | 800.00 | | | | | | | |
| **IMPERIAL'S GRAPE** | | | | | | | | | |
| Bowl, 10" – 12", ruffled | 100.00 | 225.00 | 130.00 | 400.00 | 600.00 | 275.00 | | | Lav, 275.00 |
| Bowl, 4" – 5", ruffled | 20.00 | 40.00 | 25.00 | 50.00 | | | 45.00 | | Violet, 100.00 |
| | | | | | | | | | Lav, 65.00 |
| Berry Bowl, lg. | 45.00 | 100.00 | 50.00 | | | 135.00 | 80.00 | 50.00 | MMG, 400.00 |
| | | | | | | | | | Lav, 125.00 |
| Berry Bowl, sm. | 10.00 | 30.00 | 15.00 | | | 45.00 | 20.00 | 15.00 | Vio, 225.00 |
| Bowl, 8", round deep | 20.00 | 75.00 | 25.00 | | | | 35.00 | | |
| Bowl, 8" – 9", ruffled | 35.00 | 135.00 | 45.00 | 400.00 | 5,000.00 | 225.00 | 175.00 | 45.00 | Vio, 200.00 |
| Bowl, 8" – 9", low ruffled | 65.00 | 145.00 | 55.00 | | | 200.00 | | 75.00 | Lav, 175.00 |
| Basket, handled | 100.00 | | | | 450.00 | 100.00 | | 100.00 | Lav, 225.00 |
| Compote, stemmed | 35.00 | 185.00 | 45.00 | 100.00 | | 300.00 | 85.00 | | Olive, 100.00 |
| | | | | | | | | | Aq, 175.00 |
| Cup and Saucer | 70.00 | 165.00 | 75.00 | | | | | | |
| Goblet, stemmed | 50.00 | 150.00 | 55.00 | | | | | | |
| Nappy, handled | 65.00 | 145.00 | | | | | | | |
| Nut Bowl | 125.00 | 325.00 | | | 600.00 | | | | |
| Plate, 6" | 70.00 | 275.00 | 100.00 | 900.00 | 2,000.00 | | 165.00 | | Teal, 375.00 |
| Plate, 9" | 110.00 | 2,500.00 | 175.00 | 3,000.00 | | 1,250.00 | 1,000.00 | 100.00 | Aq, 650.00 |
| Punch Bowl and Base | 175.00 | 1,800.00 | 275.00 | | | | 750.00 | | M/Bl, 350.00 |
| Punch Cup | 20.00 | 65.00 | 25.00 | | | | 50.00 | | |
| Rose bowl | 400.00 | 1,100.00 | 350.00 | | | | 700.00 | | |
| Spittoon | 2,000.00 | | 2,500.00 | | | | | | |
| Water Carafe | 200.00 | 225.00 | 150.00 | 300.00 | | 550.00 | | | Aq, 275.00 |
| Water Pitcher | 100.00 | 500.00 | 150.00 | 1,500.00 | | 400.00 | 675.00 | | Aq, 425.00 |
| | | | | | | | | | Vio, 375.00 |
| Tumbler | 20.00 | 60.00 | 40.00 | 250.00 | | 100.00 | 125.00 | | Horehound, 75.00 |
| | | | | | | | | | Aq, 100.00 |
| Wine Decanter | 100.00 | 250.00 | 135.00 | 325.00 | | 300.00 | | 125.00 | |
| Wine, stemmed | 18.00 | 35.00 | 22.00 | 150.00 | 200.00 | 65.00 | | 25.00 | Olive, 50.00 |
| | | | | | | | | | M/Bl, 40.00 |
| Salver, 8½" | 225.00 | | | | | | | | |
| **IMPERIAL'S GRAPE VARIANT** | | | | | | | | | |
| Bowl, 7½" | 50.00 | | | | | | | | |
| **LITTLE BARREL** | | | | | | | | | |
| Barrel Bottle | 150.00 | | 135.00 | | | 175.00 | | | |
| **LOGANBERRY** | | | | | | | | | |
| Vase, 10" | 250.00 | 1,275.00 | 350.00 | 1,000.00 | | 1,000.00 | 750.00 | | |
| Vase, flared top | | | | | | | 650.00 | | |
| Vase, ball top | | 2,500.00 | | | | | | | |

| | MARI | PURPLE | HELIOS | EMERALD | COBALT | SMOKE | AMBER | CLAM | OTHERS |
|---|---|---|---|---|---|---|---|---|---|
| **LONG HOBSTAR** | | | | | | | | | |
| Bowl, 8" – 9" | 35.00 | 200.00 | 125.00 | | | | | | |
| Bride's Bowl/Holder | 80.00 | 250.00 | 150.00 | | | | | | |
| Fruit Bowl and Base | 85.00 | 500.00 | 225.00 | | | 250.00 | | | |
| **LUSTRE ROSE AND OPEN ROSE** | | | | | | | | | |
| Berry Bowl, lg. | 45.00 | 150.00 | 65.00 | | 375.00 | 275.00 | 85.00 | | Vas, 250.00 Aq, 125.00 |
| Berry Bowl, sm. | 12.00 | 35.00 | 20.00 | | 125.00 | 60.00 | 25.00 | | Aq, 35.00 |
| Bowl, 7" – 8", round | 28.00 | 100.00 | 35.00 | | | 75.00 | 40.00 | | |
| Bowl, 7½" – 9", ruffled | 45.00 | 175.00 | 50.00 | 250.00 | | 175.00 | 65.00 | 35.00 | Lav, 250.00 Vas, 135.00 M/Bl, 70.00 |
| Bowl, 6", ruffled | 15.00 | 55.00 | 28.00 | | 125.00 | | 40.00 | | |
| Bowl, 8" – 9", footed | 40.00 | 150.00 | 55.00 | | 275.00 | 175.00 | 100.00 | 40.00 | Olive, 135.00 Vas, 200.00 |
| Centerpiece Bowl | 165.00 | 650.00 | 200.00 | | | 275.00 | 200.00 | 150.00 | |
| Fruit Bowl, lg. ftd. | 65.00 | 575.00 | 175.00 | | | 225.00 | | 50.00 | R, 3,200.00 Aq, 300.00 Vas, 275.00 |
| Fruit bowl, 11" – 12", collar base | 95.00 | 700.00 | 200.00 | | | 275.00 | | | |
| Butter Dish | 90.00 | 375.00 | 150.00 | | | | 250.00 | | M/Bl, 150.00 Teal, 300.00 |
| Creamer or Spooner | 35.00 | 95.00 | 45.00 | | | | 75.00 | | M/Bl, 75.00 Teal, 100.00 |
| Covered Sugar | 50.00 | 125.00 | 50.00 | | | | 90.00 | | M/Bl, 90.00 Teal, 150.00 |
| Fernery, footed | 45.00 | 250.00 | 100.00 | | 165.00 | 200.00 | 150.00 | 40.00 | Amberina, 750.00 W, 325.00 |
| Plate, 9" | 100.00 | 2,200.00 | 165.00 | | | | 350.00 | 125.00 | Lime, 200.00 Aq, 275.00 |
| Plate, whimsey ftd. | 250.00 | | | | | | | | |
| Rose bowl | 75.00 | 500.00 | 110.00 | | | 300.00 | 100.00 | | |
| Water Pitcher | 125.00 | 850.00 | 250.00 | | | | 400.00 | | M/Bl, 175.00 |
| Tumbler, ribbed int. | 25.00 | 100.00 | 40.00 | | | 150.00 | 100.00 | | Olive, 100.00 Aq, 125.00 |
| Water Pitcher, var. | 135.00 | | | | | | | 150.00 | |
| Tumbler, variant | 30.00 | | | | | | | 35.00 | W, 325.00 Teal, 150.00 Aq, 125.00 |
| Whimsey Vase | | | | | | | | 225.00 | M/Bl, 500.00 |
| **MORNING GLORY** | | | | | | | | | |
| Vase, 3" – 4½" | 65.00 | 150.00 | 85.00 | 200.00 | | 140.00 | | | |
| Vase, 5" – 7" | 35.00 | 125.00 | 65.00 | 145.00 | 200.00 | 150.00 | | | Olive, 90.00 |
| Vase, 8" – 12" | 60.00 | 135.00 | 80.00 | 165.00 | 225.00 | 165.00 | | | M/Bl, 150.00 |
| Vase, JIP shape | 65.00 | 225.00 | | 300.00 | | 225.00 | | | |
| Vase, 13" – 16", mid size | 165.00 | 325.00 | 175.00 | 400.00 | | 500.00 | | | |
| Vase, 17" – 19", funeral | 225.00 | 350.00 | 200.00 | 475.00 | | 325.00 | 500.00 | | |
| **NUCUT #537** | | | | | | | | | |
| Jelly Compote, 4½" | 175.00 | | | | | | | | |

| | MARI | PURPLE | HELIOS | EMERALD | COBALT | SMOKE | AMBER | CLAM | OTHERS |
|---|---|---|---|---|---|---|---|---|---|
| **NUMBER #5** | | | | | | | | | |
| Bowl, 7" – 9" | 75.00 | | | | | 135.00 | | | |
| Celery Vase, 6" | 200.00 | | | | | | | | |
| **OCTAGON** | | | | | | | | | |
| Berry Bowl, lg. | 40.00 | 150.00 | 75.00 | | | | | | |
| Berry Bowl, sm. | 15.00 | 35.00 | 25.00 | | | | | | |
| Bowl, lg., 10" – 12" | 60.00 | 225.00 | 100.00 | | | | | | IB, 75.00 |
| Butter Dish | 200.00 | 500.00 | 200.00 | | | | | | Aq, 350.00 |
| Creamer or Spooner | 50.00 | 175.00 | 90.00 | | | | | | Aq, 100.00 |
| Covered Sugar | 75.00 | 200.00 | 100.00 | | | | | | Aq, 125.00 |
| Compote, large | 75.00 | 275.00 | | | | | | | |
| Compote, small, 5" | 100.00 | 300.00 | | | | | | | Teal, 250.00 |
| Cordial, stemmed | 250.00 | | | | | | | | Aq, 350.00 |
| Goblet, stemmed | 40.00 | | | | | | 85.00 | | M/Bl, 85.00 |
| Nappy, handled | 150.00 | | | | | | | | |
| Milk Pitcher | 85.00 | 400.00 | | | | | | | |
| Punch Cup | 45.00 | | | | | | | | |
| Salt and Pepper, pair | 300.00 | 500.00 | | | | | | | |
| Sherbet | 75.00 | | | | | | | | |
| Toothpick Holder | 175.00 | 400.00 | | | | | | | |
| Water Pitcher, 8" | 90.00 | 1,600.00 | | | | | | | |
| Water Pitcher, lg. | 165.00 | 950.00 | | | | | | | |
| Tumbler, ground base | 25.00 | | | | | | | | |
| Tumbler, collar base | 30.00 | 85.00 | 150.00 | | | 300.00 | | | Olive, 175.00<br>Teal, 225.00 |
| Vase, 8", ped. ftd. | 100.00 | | | | | | | 100.00 | |
| Wine Decanter | 85.00 | 650.00 | 750.00 | | | | | | |
| Wine, stemmed | 20.00 | 100.00 | 150.00 | | | | | 40.00 | Aq, 250.00<br>W, 425.00 |
| **OPTIC AND BUTTONS** | | | | | | | | | |
| Bowl, 5", round | 22.00 | | | | | | | 20.00 | |
| Bowl, 8", round | 25.00 | | | | | | | 20.00 | |
| Bowl, 2-Handled | 35.00 | | | | | | | 35.00 | |
| Cup and Saucer | 300.00 | | | | | | | 200.00 | |
| Goblet, stemmed | 65.00 | | | | | | | 50.00 | |
| Nut Cup, 2-handled | 150.00 | | | | | | | | |
| Open Salt, 2-handled | 175.00 | | | | | | | | |
| Plate, 6" | 65.00 | | | | | 125.00 | | 50.00 | |
| Plate, 7½" | 50.00 | | | | | 165.00 | | 40.00 | |
| Plate, 9" | 75.00 | | | | | | | | |
| Rose bowl | 75.00 | | | | | | | 65.00 | |
| Stemmed Compote | 50.00 | | | | | | | 45.00 | Lav, 75.00 |
| Water Pitcher | 475.00 | | | | | | | 250.00 | |
| Tumbler | 65.00 | | | | | | | 50.00 | |
| Wine, stemmed | 75.00 | | | | | | | 75.00 | |
| **OPTIC FLUTE** | | | | | | | | | |
| Bowl, 8" – 9" | 25.00 | 60.00 | | | | 50.00 | | 20.00 | |
| Bowl, 5" – 6" | 10.00 | 20.00 | | | | 20.00 | | 10.00 | |
| Compote | 25.00 | 100.00 | | | | 50.00 | | 20.00 | |
| Spittoon, stemmed | 300.00 | | | | | | | | |

| | MARI | PURPLE | HELIOS | EMERALD | COBALT | SMOKE | AMBER | CLAM | OTHERS |
|---|---|---|---|---|---|---|---|---|---|
| **OVAL AND ROUND** | | | | | | | | | |
| Bowl, 8" – 9½" | 30.00 | 80.00 | 50.00 | | | | 60.00 | | |
| Bowl, 5" – 6" | 8.00 | 25.00 | 18.00 | | | | 20.00 | | |
| Chop Plate, 10" – 11" | 300.00 | | | | | | 450.00 | | |
| Rose bowl | 165.00 | | | | | | | | |
| **PANSY** | | | | | | | | | |
| Bowl, 8" – 9½", ruffled | 45.00 | 145.00 | 75.00 | | | 175.00 | 125.00 | 75.00 | Lav, 135.00 |
| Bowl, 9½", low ruffled | 55.00 | 165.00 | 85.00 | | | 200.00 | 140.00 | 85.00 | Lav, 175.00 |
| Creamer or Sugar | 25.00 | 55.00 | 30.00 | | | | 35.00 | 30.00 | Aq, 40.00 |
| Dresser Tray, oval | 100.00 | 225.00 | 110.00 | | | | 145.00 | 90.00 | |
| Nappy, handled | 30.00 | 100.00 | 25.00 | | | 55.00 | 45.00 | 30.00 | |
| Pickle Dish, oval | 35.00 | 100.00 | 50.00 | | 225.00 | 120.00 | 75.00 | 35.00 | IB, 400.00 |
| **PARLOR PANELS** | | | | | | | | | |
| Vase, squat, 4" | 100.00 | 175.00 | | | 1,750.00 | 200.00 | | | |
| Vase, 5" – 7" | 70.00 | 100.00 | | | | 150.00 | | | |
| Vase, 8" – 12" | 65.00 | 195.00 | 125.00 | | | 165.00 | 125.00 | | |
| Vase, 13" – 15" | 125.00 | 175.00 | 135.00 | | | 250.00 | 200.00 | | Honey Amb, 275.00 |
| Vase, 17", funeral | 250.00 | | | | | | | | |
| **PILLAR FLUTE** | | | | | | | | | |
| Bowl, 10", round | 25.00 | | | | | 45.00 | | 20.00 | |
| Bowl, 6", round | 10.00 | | | | | 15.00 | | 5.00 | |
| Bowl, 6", square | 20.00 | | | | | | | 15.00 | |
| Celery Tray, oval | 25.00 | | | | | 40.00 | | 20.00 | |
| Compote | 30.00 | | | | | 45.00 | | 20.00 | |
| Console set, 3 pc. | 50.00 | | | | | | | 45.00 | R, 150.00 |
| Creamer or Sugar | 18.00 | | | | | 40.00 | | 15.00 | R, 75.00 |
| Pickle Dish, oval | 20.00 | | | | | | | 15.00 | |
| Plate, 7½", round | 40.00 | | | | | | | 30.00 | |
| Plate, 6", square | 45.00 | | | | | | | 35.00 | |
| Rose bowl | 35.00 | | | | | | | 30.00 | |
| Salt and Pepper, pair | 75.00 | | | | | | | 75.00 | |
| Water Pitcher | 80.00 | | | | | | | 70.00 | |
| Tumbler | 35.00 | | | | | | | 30.00 | |
| Vase, 8", ped. ftd. | 45.00 | | | | | 75.00 | | 35.00 | |
| **PLAIN JANE** | | | | | | | | | |
| Bowl, 7" – 9" | 20.00 | 55.00 | 35.00 | | | 35.00 | | | |
| Bowl, 4" – 6" | 5.00 | 25.00 | 18.00 | | | 15.00 | | | |
| Basket, handled | 50.00 | 100.00 | | | | 85.00 | | | W, 100.00 |
| | | | | | | | | | Aq, 85.00 |
| | | | | | | | | | IG, 150.00 |
| **POINSETTIA** | | | | | | | | | |
| Milk Pitcher | 55.00 | 2,000.00 | 400.00 | 1,200.00 | | 300.00 | | | Lav, 300.00 |
| **POPPY SHOW** | | | | | | | | | |
| Vase, 12" | 725.00 | 4,200.00 | 1,500.00 | | | 3,500.00 | 7,500.00 | 1,150.00 | PM, 1,000.00 |
| Hurricane Lamp | | 4,500.00 | | | | | | | |
| Table Lamp, Elec. | 3,000.00 | | | | | | | | |
| **PREMIUM** | | | | | | | | | |
| Candlesticks, pair | 55.00 | 200.00 | 125.00 | | | 150.00 | 175.00 | 50.00 | Cel Bl, 100.00 |
| **PROPELLOR** | | | | | | | | | |
| Compote, small | 30.00 | 200.00 | 75.00 | 100.00 | | 125.00 | | | |

| | MARI | PURPLE | HELIOS | EMERALD | COBALT | SMOKE | AMBER | CLAM | OTHERS |
|---|---|---|---|---|---|---|---|---|---|
| Compote, lg., 8" – 9" | 125.00 | | | | | | | | |
| Vase, 7½", stemmed | 100.00 | | | | | | | | |
| **RANGER** | | | | | | | | | |
| Bowl, 6" – 9" | 45.00 | | | | | | | 40.00 | |
| Creamer or Sugar | 50.00 | | | | | | | | |
| Sherbet, ped. ftd. | 50.00 | | | | | | | | |
| Water Pitcher | 350.00 | | | | | | | | |
| Tumbler | 300.00 | | | | | | | | |
| Vase, 8", ped. ftd. | 100.00 | | | | | 175.00 | | | |
| **RIPPLE** | | | | | | | | | |
| Vase, squat, 5" – 7" | 55.00 | 125.00 | 50.00 | | | | 100.00 | 45.00 | Lav, 150.00 |
| Vase, 8" – 12", standard | 28.00 | 100.00 | 50.00 | 225.00 | 350.00 | 175.00 | 90.00 | 35.00 | W, 225.00 |
| | | | | | | | | | Lav, 200.00 |
| | | | | | | | | | Aq, 150.00 |
| | | | | | | | | | Vio, 165.00 |
| | | | | | | | | | Teal, 250.00 |
| | | | | | | | | | R, 750.00 |
| | | | | | | | | | Olive, 175.00 |
| Vase, 13" – 16", mid sz. | 75.00 | 175.00 | 100.00 | | | | 225.00 | 100.00 | Lav, 325.00 |
| | | | | | | | | | Vio, 375.00 |
| | | | | | | | | | Teal, 275.00 |
| Vase, 17" – 21", funeral | 200.00 | 375.00 | 175.00 | | | | | 175.00 | Teal, 425.00 |
| **ROBIN** | | | | | | | | | |
| Mug | 75.00 | | | | | 275.00 | | | M/GR, 150.00 |
| | | | | | | | | | M/Smoke, 200.00 |
| Water Pitcher | 200.00 | | | | | | | | |
| Tumbler | 40.00 | | | | | 350.00 | | | |
| **ROCOCO** | | | | | | | | | |
| Bowl, 5" – 6", dome ftd. | 40.00 | | | | | 75.00 | | | |
| Bowl, 9", dome ftd. | 95.00 | | | | | | | | |
| Vase, 5" – 6" | 110.00 | | | | | 235.00 | | | Lav, 200.00 |
| **ROYALTY** | | | | | | | | | |
| Fruit Bowl and Base | 175.00 | | | | | 325.00 | | | |
| Punch Bowl and Base | 350.00 | | | | | | | | |
| Punch Cup | 35.00 | | | | | | | | |
| **SCROLL AND FLOWER PANELS** | | | | | | | | | |
| Vase, 10" | 450.00 | 1,000.00 | | | | | | | |
| **SCROLL EMBOSSED** | | | | | | | | | |
| Bowl, 4" – 5", File ext. | 30.00 | 55.00 | | | | 100.00 | | | Lav, 65.00 |
| Bowl, 6" – 7", File ext. | 45.00 | 75.00 | | | | 135.00 | | | |
| Bowl, 8" – 9½", File ext. | 50.00 | 125.00 | | | | 175.00 | | | Lav, 135.00 |
| Bowl, 7" – 9", Plain ext. | 40.00 | 90.00 | 55.00 | | | 125.00 | | 45.00 | Aq, 70.00 |
| Bowl, 8" – 9" Hobstar and Tassels ext. | 150.00 | 300.00 | | | | | | | Teal, 250.00 |
| Compote, Curved Star ext. | 48.00 | 225.00 | 100.00 | | | | | | Vas, 200.00 |
| Compote, plain ext. | 40.00 | 160.00 | 48.00 | | | | 100.00 | | Aq, 75.00 |
| Compote, miniature | 200.00 | 375.00 | | | | | | | Lav, 250.00 |
| Goblet | | | 75.00 | | | | | | |
| Nut Dish | | 200.00 | | | | | | | |
| Sherbet | | 125.00 | | | | | | | |

| | MARI | PURPLE | HELIOS | EMERALD | COBALT | SMOKE | AMBER | CLAM | OTHERS |
|---|---|---|---|---|---|---|---|---|---|
| **SCROLL EMBOSSED, cont.** | | | | | | | | | |
| Plate, 9" | 200.00 | 425.00 | 145.00 | | | | | | Aq, 225.00 |
| **SHELL (AND SAND)** | | | | | | | | | |
| Bowl, 6" – 7" | 75.00 | 200.00 | 80.00 | | | | | | |
| Bowl, 8" – 9" | 100.00 | 350.00 | 100.00 | | | 200.00 | 250.00 | | |
| Plate, 9" | 300.00 | 1,200.00 | 375.00 | 650.00 | | 875.00 | | | Aq, 375.00 |
| **SIX-SIDED** | | | | | | | | | |
| Candlesticks, Pair | 400.00 | 1,300.00 | 350.00 | | | 900.00 | | | |
| **SMOOTH PANELS** | | | | | | | | | |
| Vase, 5" – 12" | 35.00 | 75.00 | | | | 100.00 | | 30.00 | R, 300.00 |
| | | | | | | | | | MMG, 100.00 |
| | | | | | | | | | SM/MG, 250.00 |
| | | | | | | | | | IC, 60.00 |
| | | | | | | | | | Teal, 125.00 |
| Rose bowl | 35.00 | | | | | | | 30.00 | W, 75.00 |
| | | | | | | | | | Teal, 125.00 |
| **SMOOTH RAYS** | | | | | | | | | |
| Bowl, 9", flared | 25.00 | 45.00 | | | | 50.00 | | 20.00 | |
| Bowl, 10", straight | 30.00 | | | | | | | 25.00 | Teal, 40.00 |
| Champagne, 6 oz. | 45.00 | | | | | | | 45.00 | |
| Claret, 4 oz. | 45.00 | | | | | | | 45.00 | |
| Cordial, 1 oz. | 100.00 | | | | | | | 100.00 | |
| Custard Cup | 15.00 | | | | | | | 10.00 | |
| Goblet, either size | 30.00 | | | | | | | 30.00 | |
| Plate, 8" | 30.00 | | | | | | | 25.00 | Teal, 45.00 |
| Plate, 12" | 45.00 | | | | | | | 40.00 | Teal, 75.00 |
| Rose bowl | 40.00 | | | | | | | 30.00 | W, 75.00 |
| Sherbet, stemmed | 10.00 | | | | | | | 8.00 | |
| Water Pitcher | 50.00 | | | | | | | | |
| Tumbler | 15.00 | | | | | | | | |
| Wine, 2 oz. | 40.00 | | | | | | | 40.00 | |
| Wine, 3 oz. | 45.00 | | | | | | | 45.00 | |
| **SNOW FANCY** | | | | | | | | | |
| Bowl, 5" – 6" | 35.00 | 75.00 | 50.00 | | | | | | W, 80.00 |
| Creamer or Spooner | 65.00 | | | | | | | | |
| **SODA GOLD** | | | | | | | | | |
| Candlesticks, pair | 55.00 | | | | | 75.00 | | | |
| Console Bowl | 45.00 | | | | | 75.00 | | | |
| Chop Plate, 11" – 12" | 75.00 | | | | | | | | |
| Salt and Pepper, pair | 100.00 | | | | | 125.00 | | | Aq, 225.00 |
| Water Pitcher | 150.00 | | | | | 225.00 | | | |
| Tumbler | 40.00 | | | | | 60.00 | | | |
| **SPIRAL** | | | | | | | | | |
| Candlesticks, pair | 100.00 | | 135.00 | | | 165.00 | | | |
| **STAR AND FILE** | | | | | | | | | |
| Bowl, 7" – 8", round | 35.00 | | | | | | | | |
| Bowl, 7" – 8", square | 35.00 | | | | | | | | |
| Bowl, 7" – 8", two-hdld. | 30.00 | | | | | | | | |
| Celery Vase, 2-hdld. | 60.00 | | | | | | | | |
| Champagne, stemmed | 90.00 | | | | | | | | |

| | MARI | PURPLE | HELIOS | EMERALD | COBALT | SMOKE | AMBER | CLAM | OTHERS |
|---|---|---|---|---|---|---|---|---|---|
| **STAR AND FILE, cont.** | | | | | | | | | |
| Compote | 40.00 | | | | | | | 30.00 | |
| Cordial, 1 oz. | 275.00 | | | | | | | | |
| Creamer or Sugar | 30.00 | | | | | | | | |
| Custard Cup | 40.00 | | | | | | | | |
| Goblet, stemmed | 50.00 | | | | | | | | |
| Ice Cream, stemmed | 75.00 | | | | | | | | |
| Plate, 6½" | 150.00 | | | | | | | | |
| Relish, oval, 2-hdld. | 30.00 | | | | | | | | |
| Rose bowl | 75.00 | 250.00 | 150.00 | | | | 175.00 | | IG, 300.00 |
| Sherbet, stemmed | 40.00 | | | | | | | | |
| Water Pitcher | 225.00 | | | | | | | | |
| Tumbler, 4¼" | 50.00 | | | | | | | | |
| Tumbler, 4¾", ice tea | 175.00 | | | | | | | | |
| Tumbler, Juice | 200.00 | | | | | | | | |
| Wine Decanter | 165.00 | | | | | | | | |
| Wine, stemmed | 45.00 | | | | | | | | |
| Nut bowl, 5" | 75.00 | | | | | | | | |
| **STAR MEDALLION** | | | | | | | | | |
| Bowl, 6" – 7½", round | 25.00 | | | | | 40.00 | | 20.00 | |
| Bowl, 6" – 7½", square | 30.00 | | | | | 45.00 | | 25.00 | |
| Bowl, dome ftd. | 40.00 | | | | | | | | |
| Celery Vase, ped. ftd. | 85.00 | | | | | 125.00 | | 85.00 | |
| Custard Cup | 25.00 | | | | | | | | |
| Compote | 35.00 | | | | | | | 35.00 | |
| Goblet, stemmed | 45.00 | | | | | 80.00 | | | |
| Milk Pitcher | 35.00 | | | | | 90.00 | | 30.00 | |
| Plate, 6" – 7½" | 45.00 | | | | | | | | |
| Plate, 9½" | 65.00 | | | | | 100.00 | | 50.00 | |
| Tumbler, 4" | 25.00 | | | | | 60.00 | | | |
| Tumbler, lemonade | 35.00 | | | | | 60.00 | | | |
| **STAR OF DAVID** | | | | | | | | | |
| Bowl, 8" – 9½" | 135.00 | 235.00 | 125.00 | | | 350.00 | | | |
| Bowl, 7" – 8", round | 225.00 | 400.00 | | | | | | | |
| **STAR SPRAY** | | | | | | | | | |
| Bowl, 7½", round | 35.00 | | | | | 50.00 | | | |
| Bride's Bowl and Holder | 75.00 | | | | | 100.00 | | | |
| Plate, 7½" | | | | | | 100.00 | | | |
| **SWIRL** | | | | | | | | | |
| Vase, 7" – 8" | 15.00 | | | | | 20.00 | | 10.00 | W, 35.00 |
| **SWIRL RIB** | | | | | | | | | |
| Bowl, 5" – 9" | 15.00 | | | | | | | | |
| Candlesticks, pair | 30.00 | | | | | | | | |
| Creamer or Sugar | 15.00 | | | | | | | | |
| Cup and Saucer | 45.00 | | | | | | | | |
| Mug | 50.00 | | | | | | | | |
| Plate, 6" | 15.00 | | | | | | | 10.00 | |
| Plate, 8" – 9" | 25.00 | | | | | | | | |
| Server, center hdld. | 30.00 | | | | | | | | |
| Sherbet | 10.00 | | | | | | | 10.00 | |

| | MARI | PURPLE | HELIOS | EMERALD | COBALT | SMOKE | AMBER | CLAM | OTHERS |
|---|---|---|---|---|---|---|---|---|---|
| **THIN RIB AND DRAPE** | | | | | | | | | |
| Vase, 4" – 7" | 85.00 | 225.00 | 145.00 | | 500.00 | | | | Cel Bl, 300.00 |
| **THREE IN ONE** | | | | | | | | | |
| Bowl, 8" – 9" | 30.00 | 75.00 | 50.00 | | | | 100.00 | 25.00 | |
| Bowl, 4" – 5" | 10.00 | 40.00 | 30.00 | | | | 45.00 | 10.00 | |
| Bowl, 6" – 7" | 10.00 | 45.00 | 30.00 | | | | 55.00 | 10.00 | |
| Plate, 6" – 7" | 125.00 | | | | | | | | |
| Rose bowl | 75.00 | | | | | | | | |
| Toothpick Holder | 135.00 | | 75.00 | | | | | | |
| **THREE ROW** | | | | | | | | | |
| Vase, 8" | 3,500.00 | 3,000.00 | | | | 4,000.00 | | | |
| Vase, Two Row var. | 3,000.00 | 2,500.00 | | | | | | | |
| **THUMBPRINT AND OVAL** | | | | | | | | | |
| Vase, 5" – 6" | 375.00 | 800.00 | | | | | | | |
| **TIGER LILY** | | | | | | | | | |
| Water Pitcher | 175.00 | 1,000.00 | 250.00 | | | | | | Olive, 300.00 Aq, 325.00 Teal, 375.00 |
| Tumbler | 35.00 | 125.00 | 45.00 | | | 375.00 | | | Olive, 100.00 Vio, 200.00 |
| **TREE BARK** | | | | | | | | | |
| Berry Bowl, lg. | 10.00 | | | | | | | | |
| Berry Bowl, sm. | 5.00 | | | | | | | | |
| Candlesticks, pair | 30.00 | | | | | | | | |
| Water Pitcher, ovoid | 100.00 | | | | | | | | |
| Water Pitcher, tank. | 30.00 | 200.00 | | | | | | | Aq, 65.00 |
| Tumbler | 5.00 | | | | | | | | Aq, 10.00 |
| Plate, 7" – 8" | 15.00 | | | | | | | | |
| Vase, cone shape | 15.00 | | | | | | | | |
| Vase, ovoid | 10.00 | | | | | | | | |
| **TULIP AND CANE** | | | | | | | | | |
| Bowl, dome ftd. | 45.00 | | | | | 65.00 | | | |
| Claret, 4 oz. | 175.00 | | | | | | | | |
| Cordial, 1½ oz. | 250.00 | | | | | | | | |
| Goblet, 8 oz. | 55.00 | | | | | | | | |
| Vase, whimsey | 90.00 | | | | | | | | |
| Wine, 3 oz. | 75.00 | | | | | | | | |
| **TWINS** | | | | | | | | | |
| Berry Bowl, 9" – 10" | 35.00 | | 100.00 | | | 175.00 | | | |
| Berry Bowl, 5" – 6" | 10.00 | | 28.00 | | 350.00 | 55.00 | | | |
| Bride's Bowl/Holder | 100.00 | | | | | | | | |
| Fruit Bowl and Base | 65.00 | | | | | 175.00 | | | |
| **TWO-HANDLED** | | | | | | | | | |
| Vase, 7" – 8", four shapes | 80.00 | | | | | 125.00 | | | W, 125.00 |
| Vase, swirled int. | 100.00 | | | | | 125.00 | | | |
| Candlestick Server | 85.00 | | | | | 100.00 | | | |
| **VINTAGE** | | | | | | | | | |
| Center Hdld. Server | 35.00 | | | | | 40.00 | | 30.00 | |
| **WAFFLE BLOCK** | | | | | | | | | |
| Basket, handled | 125.00 | | | | | | | 35.00 | Teal, 225.00 |

| | MARI | PURPLE | HELIOS | EMERALD | COBALT | SMOKE | AMBER | CLAM | OTHERS |
|---|---|---|---|---|---|---|---|---|---|
| **WAFFLE BLOCK, cont.** | | | | | | | | | |
| Bowl, 7" – 9" | 30.00 | | | | | | | 25.00 | |
| Bowl, 7" – 9", square | 40.00 | | | | | | | | |
| Creamer or Sugar | 30.00 | | | | | | | 25.00 | |
| Parfait, stemmed | 45.00 | | | | | | | 45.00 | |
| Punch Bowl and Base | 125.00 | | | | | | | 100.00 | Teal, 225.00 |
| Punch Cup | 30.00 | | | | | | | 25.00 | |
| Plate, 6" | 65.00 | | | | | | | 45.00 | |
| Rose bowl | 75.00 | | | | | | | 75.00 | |
| Salt and Pepper, pair | 100.00 | | | | | | | | |
| Spittoon | 350.00 | | | | | | | | |
| Water Pitcher | 225.00 | | | | | | | 175.00 | |
| Tumbler, collar base | 175.00 | | | | | | | 160.00 | |
| Tumbler, ground base | | | | | | | | 160.00 | |
| Vase, 10" | 100.00 | | | | | | | | |
| **WAFFLE AND HOBSTAR** | | | | | | | | | |
| Baster, handled | 200.00 | | | | | | | | |
| **WHEELS** | | | | | | | | | |
| Bowl, 8" – 9" | 100.00 | | | | 350.00 | | | | |
| **WHIRLING STAR** | | | | | | | | | |
| Bowl, 9" – 11" | 100.00 | | | | | | | | |
| Compote, Jelly | 125.00 | | | | | | | | |
| Punch Bowl and Base | 300.00 | | | | | | | | |
| Punch Cup | 30.00 | | | | | | | | |
| **WIDE PANEL** | | | | | | | | | |
| Bowl, 9" | 25.00 | | | | | 40.00 | | 20.00 | R, 150.00 / Teal, 55.00 / W, 65.00 |
| Bowl, 12" | 30.00 | | | | | 50.00 | | 25.00 | R, 225.00 |
| Plate, 8" | 20.00 | | | | | | | 15.00 | R, 75.00 / Teal, 75.00 / W, 75.00 / Cel Bl, 85.00 |
| Plate, 11" | 40.00 | | | | | | | 30.00 | R, 150.00 / W, 75.00 / Cel Bl, 100.00 |
| Plate, 14" | 35.00 | | | | | 65.00 | | 30.00 | |
| **WINDMILL** | | | | | | | | | |
| Bow, 8" – 9", collar base | 45.00 | 225.00 | 75.00 | 300.00 | | 125.00 | | 40.00 | MMG, 450.00 / Aq, 145.00 |
| Bowl, 4" – 5", collar base | 18.00 | 60.00 | 25.00 | 90.00 | | 45.00 | | 35.00 | Aq, 65.00 |
| Bowl, 8" – 9", footed | 45.00 | 225.00 | 65.00 | 300.00 | | 100.00 | | 40.00 | MMG, 475.00 |
| Bowl, "Double Dutch" | 45.00 | 200.00 | 65.00 | 275.00 | | 110.00 | 200.00 | | Teal, 250.00 |
| Dresser Tray, oval | 125.00 | 300.00 | 100.00 | | | | | | Aq, 175.00 |
| Milk Pitcher | 85.00 | 700.00 | 175.00 | | | 350.00 | | 120.00 | |
| Pickle Dish, oval | 50.00 | 165.00 | 75.00 | | | 125.00 | | | Lav, 150.00 / Aq, 225.00 |
| Water Pitcher | 100.00 | 1,200.00 | 250.00 | 1,500.00 | 2,000.00 | 750.00 | | | |

| | MARI | PURPLE | HELIOS | EMERALD | COBALT | SMOKE | AMBER | CLAM | OTHERS |
|---|---|---|---|---|---|---|---|---|---|
| **WINDMILL, cont.** | | | | | | | | | |
| Tumbler | 25.00 | 150.00 | 45.00 | 200.00 | 325.00 | 100.00 | | | Olive, 100.00 |
| | | | | | | | | | Teal, 200.00 |
| | | | | | | | | | Lav, 135.00 |
| **ZIPPERED HEART** | | | | | | | | | |
| Bowl, 9" – 10" | 100.00 | 225.00 | | | | | | | |
| Bowl, 5" – 6" | 25.00 | 50.00 | | | | | | | |
| Giant Rose bowl | | | | 4,500.00 | | | | | |
| Queen's Vase | | 3,500.00 | | 4,500.00 | | | | | |
| Rose bowl, 5" | 1,000.00 | | | | | | | | |
| **ZIPPER LOOP** | | | | | | | | | |
| Hand Lamp, 4" | 1,000.00 | | | | | 2,400.00 | | | |
| Hand Lamp, 5¼" dome ft. | 1,100.00 | | | | | 2,000.00 | | | |
| Lamp, stemmed, 6" – 7" | 600.00 | | | | | 750.00 | | | |
| Lamp, stemmed, 8" | 450.00 | | | | | 550.00 | | | |
| Lamp, stemmed, 9½" – 10" | 425.00 | | | | | 600.00 | | | |
| **LIGHT SHADES** | | | | | | | | | |
| AUGUST FLOWER | | | | | | | | | |
| Electric | 45.00 | | 75.00 | | | | | | |
| Gas | 60.00 | | 95.00 | | | | | | |
| BUZZ SAW | | | | | | | | | |
| Electric | 45.00 | | 75.00 | | | | 85.00 | | |
| Gas | 65.00 | | 100.00 | | | | 110.00 | | |
| COLONIAL | | | | | | | | | |
| Electric | 35.00 | | | | | | 45.00 | | |
| DIAMOND BLOCK | | | | | | | | | |
| Electric | 50.00 | | | | | | | | |
| ETCHED GREEK KEY | | | | | | | | | |
| Electric | 45.00 | | 75.00 | | | | | | |
| FINE CROSSHATCH | | | | | | | | | |
| Electric | 50.00 | | 85.00 | | | | | | |
| Gas | 75.00 | | 100.00 | | | | | | |
| IMPERIAL'S GRAPE | | | | | | | | | |
| Electric | 100.00 | | | | | | | | |
| LEAF GARDEN | | | | | | | | | |
| Electric | 40.00 | | | | | | | | W, 65.00 |
| Gas | 60.00 | | | | | | | | W, 75.00 |
| NUART DAISY | | | | | | | | | |
| Electric | 65.00 | | | | | | | | |
| Gas | 95.00 | | | | | | | | |
| NUART DRAPE | | | | | | | | | |
| Electric | 50.00 | | | | | | | | |
| Gas | 75.00 | | | | | | | | |
| NUART FOUR PANELS | | | | | | | | | |
| Electric, Square | | | | | | | | | W, 50.00 |
| NUART PLAIN | | | | | | | | | |
| Electric | 35.00 | | | | | | | | |
| NUART SPIPPLED | | | | | | | | | |
| Electric | 35.00 | | | | | | | | |

| | MARI | PURPLE | HELIOS | EMERALD | COBALT | SMOKE | AMBER | CLAM | OTHERS |
|---|---|---|---|---|---|---|---|---|---|
| **LIGHT SHADES, cont.**<br>MAYFLOWER | | | | | | | | | |
| Electric | 45.00 | | 75.00 | | | | | | |
| Gas | 65.00 | | 95.00 | | | | | | |
| PRIMROSE PANELS | | | | | | | | | |
| Electric | 30.00 | | | | | | | | |
| STARLYTE | | | | | | | | | |
| Electric | 45.00 | | 85.00 | | | | | | |
| Gas | 75.00 | | 100.00 | | | | | | |
| TORCH AND WREATH | | | | | | | | | |
| Electric | 35.00 | | | | | | | | |
| Gas | 60.00 | | | | | | | | |

# ABOUT THE AUTHOR

Carl Owen Burns has spent well over half of his 47 years collecting, buying, and selling carnival glass. He is a member of the Heart of America Carnival Glass Association, the Lincoln-Land Carnival Glass Club, the San Diego Carnival Glass Club, and the National Imperial Glass Collectors' Society. In addition to his first love, old carnival glass, he also collects Imperial ruby slag and jade slag glass which was made in the 1960s and 1970s. He is also an avid record collector, with an extensive collection of 1960s and 1970s rock, blues, and pop music. Carl's research articles have appeared in the *Heart of America Carnival Glass Association Newsletter* and the *Lincoln-Land Carnival Glass Club Newsletter*. He authored a book on Northwood's carnival glass and was one of the founding members of the New England Carnival Glass Association. His Dugan carnival glass pattern drawings appeared in the late William Heacock's *Pattern Glass Preview* publications.

He is a full-time antiques dealer, and his business, Minnah's Antiques, is well known throughout the country.

Amazingly, he still finds time to pursue other interests that include trout and salmon fishing, canoeing, and photography. He particularly enjoys photographing the abundant wildlife, especially the magnificent moose, that frequent the area around his home in the western mountains of Maine.

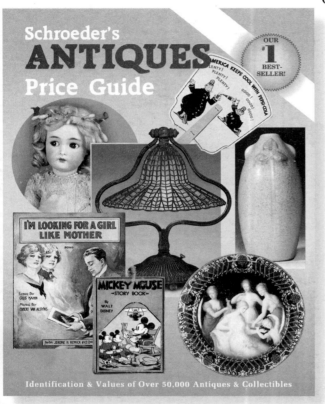